theology, ethics, implications, and possibilities
of artificial intelligence and the local church
by: rev. dr. justin r. lester

Praise for *The Church of AI:*

Anyone who has engaged Dr. Justin Lester knows that he is always ten steps ahead of everyone in the media, marketing, and ministry sector. Moreover, he is consistently in tune with the pulse of culture and the trajectory for the church's future. Here, Justin again provides a cutting-edge resource for church leaders, laypeople, and innovators. Dr. Lester does a deep dive into the history, intricacies, and implications around AI and its potential impact on church and society. This piece is not to be confused as mere pontification or creative imagination; no, Dr. Lester provides copious research around ecclesiology, theology, and technology—brilliantly nuancing each and carrying the reader to the intersection of each sphere. For Justin, Christ is ultimately found at the center. Therefore, we must explore those intersections and help our churches find comfort and fruit at that intersection. Truly, everyone who opens this rich resource will benefit significantly from the practical treasures therein.

Rev. Dr. Terrence Chandler-Harison
Senior Pastor, The Liberty Church
Clarksville, Tennessee

Rev. Lester has written a tremendous work for any pastor/ministry seeking a path forward into what is a shifting culture. He has masterfully dissected the topic of artificial Intelligence— enabling it to be approached with comfort and courage—without fear. Simply stated, every forward looking leader would benefit from this read!

Pastor Richard Gaines
Senior Pastor, Consolidated Baptist Church
Lexington, Kentucky

Dr. Justin Lester is the answer to a prayer for pastors and churches that tease out their next steps in a post-Covid world and post-Christian world. Moreover, he answers, through this work, how to harness AI to connect with our world that has grown more rapid-paced, unpredictable, and volatile. Also, any pastor who wishes to streamline and automate their church administration, while saving money and time, should read this book. No matter your age or stage of ministry, you'll learn, through reading and reflecting on this book, how to make bricks without straw, thereby transforming God's people, near and far, inside and outside the local church.

Rev. Anthony L. Trufant
Senior Pastor, Emmanuel Baptist Church
Brooklyn, NY (www.ebcconnects.com)

Dr. Justin Lester demonstrates his passion for the church while advocating for the use of technology in every facet of congregational life. Leading with head and heart for God's people, Lester's in-depth understanding of church culture and pulse on modern technological shifts elevates him as the unquestionable subject matter expert. In a world that has become increasingly dependent upon technology for creative connection and community, this book is both indisputable, indispensable, and a must-have for every strategic leader!

Dr. Eric George Vickers, Sr.
Senior Pastor, Fairfield Baptist Church
Lithonia, Georgia

Want more AI/
Follow @ThatTechPastor

DEDICATION

To the most Beautiful woman in the world.

My Baby Cakes. The Love of My life.

Court. ☺

CONTENTS

1.WHY IS THIS BOOK IMPORTANT?

COVID. Life. Changes. Acceleration.

And every other buzzword we can think of positions the church where it is now. I remember the days of "faithbook" youth Sundays, live-tweeting services, and when Instagram was for food. #Nofilter.

Then it evolved into Snapchat, Ello, Vine, and Musical.ly. Musical.ly became TikTok. COVID hit. And honestly, the world, church, business, relationships, and Gen-Z/Gen-Alpha will never be the same.

Breathe.

Our computers, phones, and Apple Vision Pro (Google Glass, anyone?) have become black mirrors. Mirrors in which we see ourselves and simultaneously seek to find ourselves. Interwoven into all of this is technology. What we use in social media, video elements, and image editing is all created by someone. While we know the ultimate creator is God in God's way, a human is writing, correcting, and evaluating the code and script essential for us to dance our lives away.

This is where Artificial Intelligence comes in. Artificial intelligence (AI) is not a new phenomenon; it has been around for years. However, recently it has been deeply invested in. As with all other forms of technology, they start in the world and enter various places of our lives. **One of the last places to adapt to technological advancement seems to be the local church.**

Always.

It does not need to be that way. The one institution that ought not to be averse to change, evaluation, movement, is the local church. Yet, our beautiful institutions are steeped in grand tradition. Pause. Have you ever considered how the traditions we hold so dear were, at one point, extremely radical?

Think about it.

A man on Passover says from here on out, "Do this in remembrance of me!" The wine you drink is my blood from now on. The bread you eat is my body from now on. Enjoy Dinner!
Jesus was exceptionally radical. Yet, the communion/eucharist practices have not been evaluated and updated, sans a few songs. To navigate this work

together, you and I must agree on this principle: Holiness is not static.

Before we jump in, I want to be clear. I LOVE the local church. I LOVE Artificial Intelligence, Augmented Reality, Virtual Reality, and everything else. I believe in the Panentheistic Nature of God; that is, everything is in God because God is in everything. So, while I will share several topics, this entire work aims to share with you why you and your ministry should use AI and New Media to share the Gospel. **The Gospel does not need help; we need help being effective with it.** There is no reason the world communicates better than the institution God created.

Should you use AI? Yes. Why? The generations and the people we are trying to reach are. Not only are we limiting our worship experiences not using AI, we are also limiting our language by not using AI. In 2024, 65% of generative AI users are Gen-Z/Millennials, a statistic that becomes even more pronounced within consumer applications like Character AI where 79 percent of its users are under 34. Three groups dominate Generative AI use: white-collar workers, Gen-z/Millennials, and Students (Gen-Alpha)…the groups absent from most churches. Professionals are using it because writing and generative AI has become great at it. It is great at crafting emails, blogs, & captions that sound authentically human. Along with that, coding is on the rise with the gen-ai tech advancing so quickly. Long story short, the groups we want in church are using it. The professions we desire to understand are using it. Church, Pastor, Leader, Influencer, I'm here to help you stop overthinking AI and embrace it!

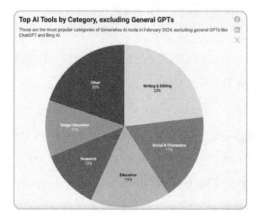

In the words of the Michael Jordan meme – Stop it. And Let me Help! With that. Let's have some fun.

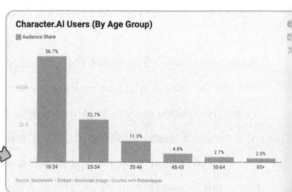

[1] Flexos. (n.d.). Generative AI: Top 150. Retrieved from https://www.flexos.work/learn/generative-ai-top-150?utm_source=www.theneurondaily.com&utm_medium=newsletter&utm_campaign=top-150-ai-tools

2. YOU ARE TECHNOLOGY

Technology is bigger than AI. Technology is bigger than social media. Technology, I argue, is You.

While this work will be intentionally focused on artificial intelligence, I want you to see yourself before we dive into it. Change and adaptation are so tricky not only because of the ease or difficulty of use; but also the disruption that comes with the process. Thus, that is the root of much of our unhappiness about new things (change, tech, evolving organizations, etc.) I want to suggest it because we are unhappy with who we are. A displaced understanding of self, limits, boundaries, and frankly, the lack of flexibility in your faith. Our displaced frustration, which could be passion to build our faith, lives, and communities, goes against movement.

We see it all over. Therefore, when things are inconvenienced or new, we return to old success. **The only thing worse than an ego built on recent success is thinking we can return to old success.** I have been there, and I am sure you have as well. Whether it is church, work, or our relationships, going "back" is far more comfortable we can soothe our ego. **Your worst enemy is not a person; it's your ego and lack of self-control!** What forbids the future is not your calloused deacons or improper members but your ego and lack of self-control!

God does not decide when to show up; we decide whether or not to see him…and you can see him in AI! What barriers do you have that have Jesus-ed Jesus out of leading you? I cannot begin to engage with technology until you destroy the barriers to adaptability and flexibility.

- What is the barrier to loving you?
- What is the barrier to you engaging fully in your identity?
- What is the barrier to you falling back in love with you?

This, my friends, is the opportunity. Why do we give Satan so much credit, especially, for tech? I have learned that what we don't understand, we demonize. Think about the annals of history where anything has changed, evolved, and grown…especially in churches. First, it's demonized, prayed over, then implemented. Whether choirs, organs, guitars, or wearing skinny jeans to preach. Our challenge is to see that we can create and innovate. Technology forces us to lean into our creativity more than our comparison.

Technology is bigger than AI.
Technology is bigger than social media.
Technology, I argue, is You.

We hate change. Because it is a challenge to the unstable. Artificial Intelligence (AI), Augmented Reality (AR), Mixed Reality (MR) Extended Reality (XR), and Virtual Reality (VR) with a lack of identity, will only lead to frustration, pain, agony, and more scowls unless what you communicate and how you show up says something different. Here are three reasons why Technology is vital to the future and sustainability of our church communities.

1. The Human Capacity to Create and Innovate

AI is a product of human ingenuity and creativity. It is a testament to our ability to think abstractly, solve problems, and create new things. AI also reflects our desire to understand the world around us and to control our destiny.

However, it is essential to remember that AI does not replace human intelligence. AI systems are still limited by the data they are trained on and the algorithms they are programmed with. They cannot think creatively or independently. Ultimately, AI is a tool that can be used for good or for evil. It is up to us to decide how we will use it.

2. God is the Ultimate Creator

The Bible teaches that God is the ultimate Creator of all intelligence, including human intelligence and AI. In Genesis 1:27, we read that God created humanity "in his image." This means we are made with the ability to think, reason, and design. We are also created with the capacity for love, compassion, and justice.

AI is a powerful tool but not a replacement for human intelligence or creativity. AI can augment our abilities, but it should not be used to replace them. We must never forget that God is the ultimate Creator of intelligence, and we are called to use our intelligence in a way that honors him.

3. The Implications of AI

The development of AI raises important questions about our understanding of humanity. Are we simply machines that are programmed to think and act? Or do we have something more?

The Bible teaches that we are more than machines. We are created in God's image, which means we have a unique capacity for love, compassion, and creativity. AI cannot replicate these qualities. Computers are not our saviors; they, too, are a part of the dust that God cursed after the fall. **We will till this Silicon Valley dust until the Lord returns (Gen 3:19).** The main challenge is our idolatry. We only seek salvation and purpose in the Father, not AI.

AI can be a powerful tool for good, but it can also be used for evil. It is up to us to decide how we will use it. We must use AI in a way that honors God and benefits all of humanity.

Our world is no less full of the idols that were present in the ancient world; ours are in our hands and sit on our desks instead of Gothic temples. As we set our hearts forward on understanding and navigating AI, let's see ourselves, rebuke any idols, and see how God is in this.

I wrote this book like a conversation. I will give as many sources as I can so that you can look up and find some other work to assist in navigating AI. Beyond the book being a conversation, Feel free to jump around. I organized it to flow, but this is more a handbook. Jump around, come back, circle and everything in between.

Lastly, when you finish, I offer an "Church of AI" masterclass online on my website **www.jrlester.com** I would love to talk to you, your church, or your community on how to engage AI. I'll gladly be the martyr.

To the future. I am proud of you for reading this.
I've prayed for you.
Thank you for existing.

3. WHAT IS ARTIFICIAL INTELLIGENCE?

Here is a concrete definition I have put together that you can use to encompass what AI is. *Artificial Intelligence (AI) is a branch of computer science that focuses on creating machines that can perform tasks that typically require human Intelligence, such as learning, problem-solving, and decision-making.* AI systems use algorithms and statistical models to analyze large amounts of data, recognize patterns, and make predictions or decisions based on that data.

Definitions of artificial Intelligence are many. Most people get their ideas about AI from the media, which leads to a popular imagination dominated by embodied AI or robots. (Minority Report anyone?) Other popular perceptions see computers as performing human-like tasks like thinking or learning. This only amplifies the perceived risks for gun-totting robots or

11

super-intelligent agents and minimizes other more realistic problems, such as algorithmic bias or lack of transparency.

History:

To understand Artificial Intelligence better, return to when it was first used. 1919! The science fiction concept, "*The Grim Game*," introduced us to a human-like robot named "Q." Continue forward, and we meet the Tin Man in *The Wizard of Oz* and Maria in *Metropolis*.

Artificial intelligence, as a term, was first introduced in 1955 by four computer and cognitive scientists: John McCarthy, Marvin Minsky, Nathaniel Rochester, and Claude Shannon.[2] The group photo shows The Dartmouth Summer Research Project on Artificial Intelligence, held in 1956, which is widely considered the event that kicked off AI as a research discipline. Those leaders regarded artificial intelligence as human intelligence precisely understood and reproduced by a computer. Their first definition of AI was the science and engineering of making intelligent machines.

As the science behind Artificial Intelligence evolved, so did the definition. What it did was stop considering

---

[2] IEEE Spectrum. (n.d.). Dartmouth AI Workshop. IEEE Spectrum.
https://spectrum.ieee.org/dartmouth-ai-workshop

human intelligence standards and see how computers could improve beyond the capacity of human brains.[3] The view of AI was that it no longer had to mimic human thinking and behavior but that it could reason better than humans with humans. From 1980 to 2000, AI research was funded, researched, and given energy. Computers were smaller and available to the public, and the researchers became business leaders who integrated their research into phones, devices, security, and robots. **AI In 1919 is a stark contrast to AI today.**

How you use it! (Sometimes without knowing)

Fast forward to today. In a world of chatbots, robots, ChatGPT, and a wide range of apps listed at the back of this book, you have used AI more than you think! If you were to try and not use AI, it would be hard to function, and  it did not just start with COVID! Remember Clippy in Microsoft Word? From form completion to predictive text messages to suggested places to eat, predictive models of AI dominate our daily lives. Here are a few ways you use AI today, sometimes without knowing it.

- **Personalized recommendations**: Online retailers and streaming services use AI to analyze user data and make customized recommendations based on user preferences.
- **Fraud detection:** Banks and credit card companies use AI to detect fraudulent transactions by analyzing large amounts of data and identifying patterns that indicate fraudulent activity.

---

[3] Rich. E & Knight, K. (1991). Artificial intelligence New Delhi: McGraw-Hill

- **Healthcare:** AI is used to assist with diagnosis and treatment planning. For example, AI algorithms can analyze medical images to detect signs of cancer or other diseases.

- **Language translation:** AI-powered language translation tools can quickly translate text or speech from one language to another, making communicating with people from different parts of the world more accessible.

- **Virtual assistants:** Virtual assistants like Siri, Alexa, and Google Assistant use AI to understand natural language and respond to user requests.

My goal is to go beyond what you know. Artificial intelligence is showcased in a myriad of ways. You may have heard of Large Language Models (LLMs), Machine Learning (ML), or Generative AI (Gen-AI), All of which lead to popular webpages such as Chat-GPT, Gemini, Claude, and various other modalities. So let's talk about them. Let's call these "Human-in-the-loop-AI."

"Human-in-the-loop-AI."

For the Machine to learn AI, there needs to be a "human-in-the-loop" to train it. Humans, you and I, are involved in training models by labeling and structuring the data, basically telling the computer what to do. Humans also test ML models, evaluating their output and rejecting errors. Thus, a virtuous loop is created where ML algorithms are trained, tested, tuned, and validated. This approach generates the best of both worlds. AI could also be the science of making computers do things that require intelligence by humans. **AI is so complex; it is computer programming that learns and adapts.**

How does AI work?

For any AI to work, it needs data. Generally, data refers to facts, numbers, words, measurements, observations, or descriptions of things. **Data** can be quantitative in numbers or qualitative in words, pictures, sounds, and symbols. **Computer software** uses quantitative data, amounts, characters, or symbols. Logical operations are performed on the data, which may be stored and transmitted as electrical signals and recorded on magnetic, optical, or mechanical recording media. Quality is what matters. **What you put in, you get out, garbage in, garbage out, quality in, quality out.** Algorithms then use this data to perform operations. **Algorithms** are pieces of software code that instruct the computer to perform a specific task. Algorithms are applied to the data. The way we categorize this data is through Machine Learning (ML) ML tells computers how to recognize patterns in data and adjust their behavior accordingly.

Most of what we have today is logic-based **Supervised Machine Learning (SML).** This type of machine learning is where humans are teachers for the computer, which later can proceed by acting autonomously. The main characteristics of artificial intelligence systems today are logic-based. They can learn based on patterns detected in the data. They can also adapt their behavior by analyzing how the environment is affected by their previous actions. The most advanced AI systems can perceive their environment through **computer vision**. Some can even communicate through natural language processing.

Neural networks: neural networks organize data into layers, starting with an input layer of raw data. Data is then transferred to the next layer, called a hidden layer. The hidden layer combines the raw data in many ways to create levels of abstraction. You can think of a pixelated image that is becoming more evident. Finally, results are produced in an output layer. Neural networks do a pretty good job of many tasks, such as powering Google image search or recognizing human handwritten digits and translating them into a digitized format.

Deep learning: Interpret relationships among data. The advantage of deep learning is that it clusters data automatically and can detect abstractions or patterns that we might not know ahead of time. This is especially useful for complicated data like unstructured text or images. A famous example is Google Translate, which has used deep learning to translate text accurately since 2016.

Diffusion models: The approach behind diffusion models is that they add more and more random noise to images. This is the diffusion process. Noise is then removed to generate the most likely novel outputs.

Neural networks and **deep learning** are both critical elements of today's AI. They function like human brains for advanced pattern recognition. Transformer architecture is central to many of today's large language models and other forms of generative AI. Transformers allow for rapid processing of context in text. Diffusion models are another critical part of generative AI. These models are just noise to generate new content, such as images.

Generative AI: This is the most forward-facing and widely accessible by the public. Think, text generation, image creation, natural speech generation, computer code production, and more.

Large language models: A specific generative AI model, often built using the transformer architecture that leverages a considerable volume of language data. Examples include models like OpenAI's GPT series. Large language models are trained on extensive text datasets and can generate coherent and contextually relevant text passages. The process of interpreting a user prompt is as follows.

Tokenization → Context Analysis → Prediction → Generation

Here is how it works technically:

Tokenization	The input text is broken down into smaller pieces called tokens. These tokens can be as short as one character or as long as one word
Context Analysis	The model looks at each token in the context of the ones around it. This is done using a mechanism called attention, which allows the model to weigh the importance of each token when predicting the next one.
Prediction	The model predicts the next token based on the context. This prediction is made by assigning probabilities to all possible following tokens and choosing the one with the highest probability
Generation	The predicted token is added to the sequence and repeated until a stop condition (like reaching a maximum length) is met

How it works for you:

Tokenization	You give an LLM a prompt.
Context Analysis	It starts processing. The encoder translates words into machine-relevant values, such as numerical vectors. It also captures semantic relationships.
Prediction	It starts outputting an answer. The transformer uses self-attention to figure out parts of the whole that are important simultaneously.
Generation	You get the answer/image, etc.

ₔ₋es of AI:

ₔeduction in Human Error: AI can significantly reduce errors and increase accuracy and precision. The decisions taken by AI are based on data and algorithms, not emotions or biases. For example, AI can perform complex surgeries with precision and accuracy, reducing the risk of human error and improving patient safety.

24/7/365 Availability: AI can work continuously without getting tired or bored. AI can handle multiple tasks simultaneously and instantly respond to queries or requests. For example, AI can provide round-the-clock customer service through chatbots or virtual assistance.

High Accuracy and Optimized Decision-Making: AI can process large amounts of data and information quickly and efficiently. AI can also analyze patterns, trends, and correlations that may be hidden or too complex for humans to understand. AI can also help make informed and rational decisions based on facts and evidence

Disadvantages of AI:

High Cost: AI requires a lot of investment in software and hardware development, maintenance, and updating. AI also consumes a lot of energy and resources to function correctly. The repairing and replacement costs of AI systems can be very high.

Lack of Creativity and Emotions: AI cannot replicate human creativity and emotions. AI cannot generate original or innovative ideas or solutions that require imagination or intuition. AI cannot understand or express emotions such as empathy, compassion, or humor. AI cannot form emotional bonds or relationships with humans.

Ethical and Social Issues: AI can pose ethical and social challenges for humans. For example, AI can raise questions about privacy, security, accountability, bias, fairness, transparency, and trust. AI can also negatively impact human values, norms, or culture.

Game Changer

Was that a lot? Great. We just scratched the surface with language that you will hear. You can read from many computer science engineers who can give more resounding technical definitions. Frankly, if you are not building a model, there is no need to know much more. But, because I love you as my audience, I put a relatively comprehensive glossary in the back of this book with some terms I mentioned. Artificial intelligence is a game changer! It has revolutionized how we live, work, and interact with technology. Here's the best way to explain it. Consider how you plan worship on Sunday.

The casual attendee only sees praise and worship, relics in prayer, the sermon, and possibly your external technology. That attendee needs to learn about the worship planning meetings, rehearsals, meetings to plan, data input, sermon preparation, volunteer training, and everything else. The same goes for AI.

While the casual explorer sees the fun online model, pictures of them as a baby or a robot, they need to see the millions of people coding data, housing memory, and learning models. While many flashy examples of AI are being used across society and businesses, even more work is being done to make AI function effortlessly across many domains. AI is no longer just a buzzword; it has become an integral part of our daily lives and will be a part of our churches.

AI is shaping our digital experiences, disrupting various industries, and has enormous potential for transformation. Take healthcare, for example. AI is used to improve diagnostics, drug discovery, and personalized medicine. Companies like Google's DeepMind have developed AI systems that detect eye diseases and cancers accurately. Self-driving cars have been a prominent application of AI in recent years. Companies like Tesla and Waymo are investing heavily in developing autonomous vehicles that could revolutionize transportation. AI-powered autonomy is not limited to cars. It can impact industries such as aviation, shipping, and logistics. AI and robotics are a powerful combination. Robots with AI capabilities are being deployed in the manufacturing, agriculture, and healthcare sectors. (We will chat about robots later) Now, what is everyone afraid of? AGI, or artificial generalized intelligence to AI systems that can outperform humans in the most economically valuable work. While we have yet to achieve AGI, many experts believe we are moving closer to this milestone.

So what? The future of AI is promising. But remember, we are in control. It is learning from what we input and what we output. **AI will not replace Humans. AI will replace the humans who don't use it!** It will continue to disrupt in ways we cannot envision today, but we can prepare today.

Q what do I **take away?**

3

"AI is no longer just a buzzword; it has become an integral part of our daily lives and will be a part of our churches."

"The future of AI is promising. But remember, we are in control."

"Artificial intelligence will not replace humans. AI will replace the humans who don't use it."

quotes to **remember**

questions to **ask**

How can we balance the advantages of AI, such as reducing errors and optimizing decision-making, with the ethical and social challenges it poses, like privacy and bias?

In what ways can our church community leverage AI to enhance our digital experiences while ensuring inclusivity and transparency?

2

Try out an image generator or LLM and use it to answer some of the questions you still have on AI.

thing to **try**

4. THEOLOGY AND AI

As I write this, my church is working with an architect to build a family fun center. Let me tell you, there are laws you did not even know existed that speak to rules and regulations down to fonts and location of the title of the building. Thank the Lord for architects. Just as those architects design a blueprint for our building, we construct frameworks to help others and ourselves digest the mystery of the gospel. In the quest to decipher the relevance of the Gospel with technology, this chapter embarks on a journey to discern the connection that Artificial Intelligence has with the gospel. In this chapter, I will answer the: *"What does it mean to frame the gospel so it can be received as good news in the world we live in today?"* To explore this, I will engage in systematic theology. Together, we will hit the intersection of faith and technology.

Theology of AI? Humanism?

"What does it mean to frame the gospel so it can be received as good news in the world we live in today?" I want to engage this using the same structure used for systematic theology for the course of Church history, God's trinitarian nature. God is Father, Son, and Holy Spirit. We believe that God sent his son, Jesus, the incarnate one, into the world as a reflection of Himself as a gift to suffer in our place as the propitiation of our sins. Those who believe in Jesus will never suffer the effects of sin (death) but are guaranteed to be with Jesus for eternity and see Him in his return (John 3:16, 16:13, Titus 3 4-7). That's the story, and I am sticking to it. Does that inform AI in any way? It does!

We know that God is the Ultimate Creator, and to encounter God is to know God. *Acts 17:14: "The God who made the world and everything in it is the Lord of heaven and earth and does not live in temples built by human hands. 25 He is not served by human hands, as if he needed anything. Instead, he gives everyone life and breath and everything else. 26 From one man he made all the nations, that they should inhabit the whole earth; and he marked out their appointed times in history and the boundaries of their lands.*

Paul is engaging with a community of people steeped in Jewish tradition with whom he could assume there is no commonality, but he found it by sharing this truth with them. God made everything. Because of that truth, we have something to talk about. **God is the creator of the humans who created Artificial intelligence.** God did not forget creation when creation inconvenienced Him. God created humanity. Humanity created Artificial Intelligence. Consider the words of Dr. Simeon Xu from the University of Edinburgh. According to Dr. Xu, human researchers are inclined to consider themselves a model of intelligence while designing AI.[4] As a result, AI tends to simulate human beings in terms of thinking processes. Despite this, AI

---

[4] Edinburgh Futures Institute. (n.d.). Understanding AI from a Theological Perspective. Retrieved from https://efi.ed.ac.uk/understanding-ai-from-a-theological-perspective/

and human beings remain fundamentally distinct due to their different natures, more so when considering human biological bodies as opposite to silicon-based systems. As such, humans and AI do not share the same moral agency.

This is the tension. Can AI be a part of your worship experience? Can AI assist in your church practices? Can AI help you in your preaching? This is going to be derived from your own moral company and perspective. Dr. Xu stated, "AI has a role to play in human morality, but what remains to be investigated is the meaning of this role."[5]

Theologically, the opportunity and issue of Artificial Intelligence comes from John Calvin's words, where he worried that our hearts are "idol factories." Technological advancements, even beyond Artificial intelligence, have bred so many people to begin to play God because AI has opened the door to far more intelligence than we knew imaginable. The below graph from Ruben Rabines details that truth.

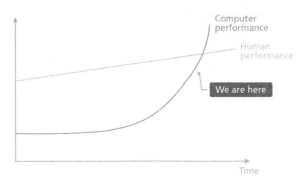

Machine learning vs. human learning
Computer performance may outpace human performance

Computer performance

Human performance

We are here

Time

---

[5] Edinburgh Futures Institute. (n.d.). Understanding AI from a Theological Perspective. Retrieved from https://efi.ed.ac.uk/understanding-ai-from-a-theological-perspective/

There is only so much that we humans can learn, but AI is learning every day. We are all searching for a "being" that is larger than ourselves and has the answers to life's questions. Whether that being is God, Santa Claus, or AI, the issue is Idol worship! This is why Paul, who was unconcerned with the church in Corinth, said: *"Some people say, quite rightly, that idols have no actual existence, that there's nothing to them, that there is no God other than our one God, that no matter how many of these so-called gods are named and worshiped they still don't add up to anything but a tall story. They say—again, quite rightly—that there is only one God, the Father, that everything comes from him, and that he wants us to live for him. Also, they say that there is only one Master—Jesus the Messiah—and that everything is for his sake, including us. Yes. It's true."* *(1 Corinthians 8:5-6 msg)* If our moral compass is not rooted in Jesus and who he is, we will continue to see a distance from the center, that is Jesus, into other areas. One such area this is evident is transhumanism.

Transhumanism

Transhumanism is where much of the discourse surrounding technology and Faith has found its landing point. Consider the words of Amy Webb, who explained the Transhumanist Movement: "Transhumant authors today sometimes announce that the process of biological evolution is itself coming to a close, and we are now entering a period of cosmological history where humans, their creations will exercise absolute control over the destiny of the universe."[6] This cannot mean much outside of what is obvious: Humanity is seeking to become her own God. It's analogous to what Yuval Noah proposed in creating a new religion called *"dataism."* Where his founding

---

[6] Amy Webb, *The Big Nine: How the Tech Titans and Their Thinking Machines Could Warp Humanity* (New York: Public Affairs, 2019) 50.

doctrine is *"Homo sapiens is an obsolete algorithm."*[7] Meaning that our purpose as humans is to process data and procreate. To prove him right, we have AI, AR, and MR. We as humans have created machines that he believes will at some time make us obsolete. Therefore, he posits, we should worship our successes. Further cementing transhumanism, Anthony Levandowski, a former employee at Google, submitted papers in California to find his religion, which worships artificial intelligence as a god.[8] His purpose statement: *"Develop and promote the realization of a Godhead based on Artificial Intelligence."* This information indeed is disparaging, but it also should encourage us! This is not a new issue, but we must address it through a firm foundation in our faith, beliefs, and understanding of God—frankly, apologetics.

Our faith has been battle-tested throughout the years against humanity's continual fight against what God created. The message of our battle is that the redemption of the Lord Jesus will never be boxed into the confines of humanity. Because of Jesus, we experience new life in Jesus (2 Peter 1:4, John 10:10). Idolatry, humanism, and the like suggests a conclusion that God's matter does not matter even though God called creation "very good" (Gen 1:31) and the resurrection brought us into the right relationship with God.

Theological Optimism

I challenge you to have a theological optimism regarding Artificial Intelligence. There are no concrete answers regarding anything in AI. Instead,

---

[7] Yuval Noah Harari, *Homo Deus: A Brief History of Tomorrow* (New York: HarperCollins, 2017), 386-387

[8] Levy, S. (2017, October 17). God Is a Bot, and Anthony Levandowski Is His Messenger. Wired. Retrieved from https://www.wired.com/story/god-is-a-bot-and-anthony-levandowski-is-his-messenger/

we are early enough where we do not have answers, yet we do know to seek and find. (Matthew 7:7). The optimism I challenge us to have is one where we understand that this moment of technology will improve our human condition, we will be closer to God, and create a world and culture that reflects how Jesus taught us to pray:

> *Our Father, Who art in heaven,*
> *Hallowed be Thy Name.*
> *Thy Kingdom come.*
> *Thy Will be done,*
> *on earth as it is in Heaven.*
> *(Matthew 6:5-15)*

We want our world, God's creation, to reflect heaven, not fight with it. God's whole intent has been to bring heaven to earth since Genesis. Sin rejected it. We, as prophetic voices, fight to reveal it! So what? We must build our character, enhance our moral standing, and strengthen our ethical foundation. How? **Trusting that since God could redeem us individually, He can use anything to redeem this world.** He started by using death and resurrection to get our attention. That's why Paul said in 2 Corinthians 5:17: *Therefore if any man is in Christ, he is a new creature: old things are passed away; behold, all things are become new.* Paul continues to say this repeatedly (Romans 6:4, 2 Cor 4 16, Gal 2:20, 6:15, Col 3:10). I use the lyrics of one of my favorite hymns to cement this. Our anchor cannot move into AI; rather, our anchor must be who Jesus is.

> *How firm a foundation, O saints of the Lord,*
> *Is laid for your faith in his excellent Word!*
> *What more can he say than to you? He has said*
> *Who unto the Savior for refuge have fled?*

AI allows us to reflect on humanity's unique capacities, such as intuition,

28

consciousness, reason, and the capacity to love. Our identity is in Jesus. Our uniqueness is in Jesus. Why? Jesus not only told us we would do greater than him (John 14) but that we are not to be distracted by anything we see because, *"I have told you these things, so that in me you may have peace. In this world you will have trouble. But take heart! I have overcome the world."* (John16:33) We are to be wise stewards of what Jesus has given us to share the message of the Gospel. The question is not if there is a theology of AI; the question is, what do you believe about Jesus, and how will you communicate it? How will you use what we have?

"Our anchor cannot move into AI; rather, Our anchor must be in who Jesus is."

"The question is not if there is a theology of AI; the question is what do you believe about Jesus and how will you communicate it?"

"We want our world, God's creation, to reflect heaven, not fight with it."

quotes to remember

questions to ask

What beliefs about Jesus inform your perspective on integrating AI into theological discourse and practice?

How can we ensure our engagement with AI reflects theological optimism and a commitment to building ethical foundations?

Consider where your faith is anchored. How healthy is your relationship with Jesus? Take time to engage with your personal devotional life before adding anything new!

thing to try

5. IS AI IN THE BIBLE?

Ok. No. But hear me out. Thus far, I have shown how our foundation is in Jesus and how AI intentionally forces us to name our motivations and ethical foundations. How can it work and apply to our churches? Paul! I love Paul if you cannot tell. I want to posit the book of Ephesians socially and culturally as a way to grapple with and utilize artificial intelligence. Paul was an innovative thinker and leader before his conversion. After his conversion, all of him was given to the gospel, ensuring that the story of Jesus reached the Gentiles. This is explained best in Philippians 3:2-7 (NIV)

2 Watch out for those dogs, those evildoers, those mutilators of the flesh. 3 For it is we who are the circumcision, serve God by his Spirit, boast in Christ Jesus, and put no confidence in the flesh— 4 though I have reasons for such confidence. If someone else thinks they have reasons to put confidence in the flesh, I have more: 5 circumcised on the eighth day, of the people of Israel, of the tribe of Benjamin, a Hebrew of Hebrews; regarding the law, a Pharisee; 6 as for zeal, persecuting the church; as for righteousness based on the law, faultless. 7 But whatever were gains to me, I now consider loss for the sake of Christ.

Paul is warning against false teachings emphasizing the true source of righteousness through faith in Christ rather than through external practices. Paul reflected on his background and achievements according to Jewish law, considering them as loss and dung compared to the value of knowing Christ. He emphasized that true righteousness comes through faith in Christ, not from following the law. Paul explained and spoke from experience that righteousness, or right standing with God, is sustained through trust in Jesus. Merging these verses with Paul's history, we can see how Philippians 3:2-7 demonstrates that Paul was an innovative thinker and leader. Paul's background as a Pharisee and his zealous adherence to the Jewish law were well-known. However, his encounter with Christ led him to rethink his understanding of righteousness and salvation radically. This transformation reflects his innovative thinking in embracing a new paradigm of faith in Christ as the basis of righteousness rather than rigidly adhering to the traditional Jewish law. Despite facing opposition and persecution, Paul's leadership in spreading this innovative message of salvation through faith in Christ further exemplifies his role as an innovative thinker and leader in the early Christian movement.

Paul was the first Facebook! Was that a stretch? Maybe. Paul was innovative in not allowing prison, opposition, persecution, or even stoning to stop him from communicating the truth about Jesus, getting them into various communities, and getting them like and subscribe. (laugh) Possibly, he was closer to YouTube. While Paul did not have social media or Artificial Intelligence, he created a new form of media that went beyond oral storytelling to ensure that his story was straightforward. He was strategic in who, what, and where he sent the story of Jesus to enact a great deal of influence because of Jesus' work through and with him. None of this is more prevalent in the Book of Ephesians. Ephesus was located on the water and was historically important, especially as a thriving port city. (See map below)

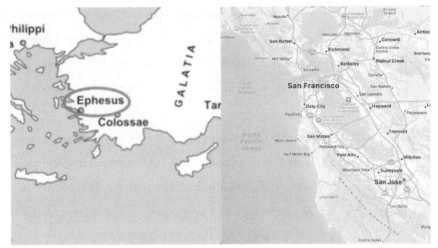

The city's access to the Aegean Sea made it a significant center for trade, contributing to its prosperity and large population. The port of Ephesus was a vital link between the East and the West, connecting Italy and Greece with Asia Minor. This strategic position facilitated the exchange of goods, ideas, and cultures, making Ephesus a cosmopolitan hub. The presence of a busy port is precisely why Paul used Ephesus to spread the gospel. As a significant trading city, Ephesus attracted people from various regions, allowing Paul to reach a diverse audience with his message.

Additionally, the city's accessibility by sea provided Paul with an efficient means to travel to and from Ephesus as he spread the teachings of Christianity throughout the region. Pause. Does this sound like Silicon Valley? San Jose is located right on the "bay" near San Francisco, where billions of dollars are exchanged regarding ideas, culture creation, and personality development.

Our lives are stored in the many servers and dollars of technological genius in one of the most biblically illiterate, unchurched, and post-Cristian areas in the country.[9] (I know, I pastor in this region) Possibly, our opportunity is like Paul's; the world created a hub of innovation, goods, ideas, and culture; we should use it to spread the gospel. He shows us how in Ephesians. (I am a preacher; you know I had to break down the scriptures at some point!)

Ephesians 2:10 - "For we are God's handiwork, created in Christ Jesus to do good works, which God prepared in advance for us to do." Just as God prepared good works in advance for believers, including the spreading of the Gospel, today, our churches can utilize technology as a tool equipped for them to fulfill their mission in the world, much like Paul leveraged Ephesus as a hub for spreading the Gospel.

Ephesians 2:19 - "Consequently, you are no longer foreigners and strangers, but fellow citizens with God's people and also members of his household." The world is diverse, and because of technology, we are incredibly interconnected. We must remember we are citizens of God's kingdom. Access to knowledge, gaining, and building with Artificial intelligence connects us across geographical, cultural, and societal boundaries, similar to how Ephesus served as a melting pot of diverse cultures and beliefs.

Ephesians 4:15-16 - "Instead, speaking the truth in love, we will grow to become in every respect the mature body of him who is the head, that is, Christ. From him, the whole body joined and held together by every supporting ligament, grows and builds itself up in love, as

---

[9] Barna Group. (2016, May 1.). Churchless Cities: Where Does Your City Rank? Retrieved from https://www.barna.com/research/churchless-cities-where-does-your-city-rank/

each part does its work." AI can assist us through translations, Language models, and other forms to speak the truth in love and to build up the body of Christ, fostering growth and unity.

Ephesians 4:29 - "Do not let any unwholesome talk come out of your mouths, but only what helps build others up according to their needs, that it may benefit those who listen." Since AI is a challenge to our morality, Paul emphasizes the importance of using technology responsibly, ensuring that our digital interactions are uplifting and edifying to others, reflecting the love and grace of Christ at all times, even online.

Ephesians 5:16 - "making the most of every opportunity, because the days are evil." Just as Paul encouraged the Ephesians to make the most of every opportunity, we can leverage technology as a powerful tool for spreading the Gospel and building community, recognizing this is a time and era we have never been in, but God is sovereign.

Ephesians 6:12 - "For our struggle is not against flesh and blood, but against the rulers, against the authorities, against the powers of this dark world and against the spiritual forces of evil in the heavenly realms." Evil is everywhere. Even online. But Christ has overcome it all. We must be mindful of the spiritual battles that occur online, recognizing that the influence of technology can be used for both good and evil. Satan is trying, but we always win.

Remember, we are to be faithful to spread the gospel. Paul was intentionally innovative in how and what he shared with broken political and religious communities. In that case, we can navigate with the anointing of the Lord to do the same! In Ephesians, Paul presents the idea of the church as a city on the water, a community of believers who are called to live a life that reflects the entire essence of God in their interactions with the world around them. In the context of emerging technologies, this concept of the church as a city on the water can be applied in several ways. Here are a few principles I want you to glean from the scriptures.

Embrace technology to spread the Gospel: Just as the early church used the Roman road system to spread the Gospel, we can use emerging technologies to reach a wider audience with the message of Jesus. This can involve using social media platforms, online courses, and other digital tools to share the Gospel with those who may not have access to traditional forms of Christian media.

Use technology to build community: The early church was characterized by its strong sense of community, which is still an essential aspect of Christian life today. New and Emerging technologies can provide new opportunities for Christians to connect and build community through online forums, virtual worship services, or other digital platforms.

Be mindful of the ethical implications of technology: As Christians engage with emerging technologies, they should be aware of the ethical implications of these technologies and how they may impact society. This can involve considering issues such as data privacy, artificial intelligence, and the potential for technology to exacerbate existing social inequalities. I give an entire chapter on Ethics later.

I want you to view technology as a means of glorifying God and serving others rather than an end in itself. Remember, Theological optimism.

> *"Follow God's example, therefore, as dearly loved children and walk in the way of love, just as Christ loved the church and gave himself up for her to make her holy, cleansing her by the washing with water through the word, and to present her to himself as a radiant church, without stain or wrinkle or any other blemish, but holy and blameless. In this same way, husbands should love their wives as their bodies. He who loves his wife loves himself. After all, no one ever hated his body, but he feeds and cares for it, just as Christ does the church, for we are members of his body. 'For this reason, a man will leave his father and mother*

and be united to his wife, and the two will become one flesh.' This is a profound mystery—but I am talking about Christ and the church." (Ephesians 5:1-20)

Jesus instructs us that we are to be faithful stewards of the resources he has entrusted us until he returns. One of those resources is technology. I refuse to believe that the God of the universe is in heaven and forgot about Artificial intelligence, new media, and social media. Technology is an opportunity for us to learn to trust God again, using technology to deal with uncertainty. Consider that in 2020, there were over three billion people - of 4 in 10 people - who had no internet access; by and large, these are the same people who have not heard the gospel.[10] Love. Create Unity. We are One Body. Use technology and other means to build up the body of Christ and spread the Gospel to those outside the church. Use tech, but do not let tech use you. Serve through tech, but do not let Tech dominate you. Appreciate tech's potential, but always remember who and what is truly worthy of worship.

In the end, our churches aim to spread the gospel by any means necessary. Would Spurgeon, who stood in an immaculate pulpit and found ways to disseminate his sermons, use AI to share his word to apply to communities beyond his reach? Would C.L. Franklin use AI to create new album covers so we know the imagery his whoop was trying to convey? Would Martin Luther King use AI to create a video of his dream for us to see while he told us he had a dream? I'm sure they would!

---

[10] For more information on those who have never heard the gospel, see
https://joshuaproject.cnet/people_groups/statistics.

Images made using imagine.meta.com

Prompt: Imagine C.H. Spurgeon Using Technology to preach in his pulpit in England. Have him using a computer or tablet.

Prompt: Generate an image depicting a scene where people of diverse backgrounds are sitting together at a table, symbolizing unity and brotherhood, set against a backdrop of rolling red hills reminiscent of Georgia's landscape.

Prompt: Generate an album cover with an Image of C.L. Franklin preaching with and Eagle Stirring her Nest (Deuteronomy 32:11)

Q what do I **take away?**

"Embrace technology as a means of glorifying God and serving others, rather than an end in itself."

"Use technology to build up the body of Christ and spread the Gospel to those outside the church."

"Serve through tech, but do not let Tech dominate you."

quotes to remember

questions to ask

How can we leverage technology to spread the Gospel effectively while remaining faithful stewards of its resources?

How can churches use technology to build community and connect with individuals who may not have access to traditional forms of Christian outreach?

How is your stewardship? Technology is an opportunity to consider your mindset of stewardship. Use it as a tool to fulfill the Great Commission.

thing to try

6. MINDSET TO LEAD CHANGE

I love BBQ, especially low-smoked beef. Yes, any cut of beef. One weekend, my family and I found a new restaurant with some of the area's best-ranked BBQs. When we were looking at the menu, I saw an option for a "Pig-out Feast." It was a burger with four patties, fries, bacon, and brisket. If you consumed the entire burger in 25 minutes, it was free. The first time we went, I did not eat it because I was not ready for that much meat in that short period. I also needed to have a driver to make sure I could sleep while throwing up after. But two weeks later, I was ready! I did not eat the day before, prepared my mind, and went to the restaurant for a free meal. Preparation made the difference.

As we navigate this book on Artificial Intelligence and the Local church, we could bring many things to the table that can assist with the growth and sustainability of our churches. The most important thing for me is not the output but your mindset. Are you mentally prepared to infuse a disruptive technology into a traditional organism? Churches are nomadic. Each of our denominations is steeped in tradition, not to mention that special tradition what makes your church "special." No matter your race, ethnicity, creed, origin, or social/physical/economic location, there is a "tradition" that you are keeping and disrupting.

Can I free you? The best definition of tradition I have heard is "frozen success." Our traditions are nothing more than a frozen period in time. We can unfreeze them once we create a new tradition. **How you frame a thing is how you engage in a thing.** Do not make the mistake of trying to make new technologies "fit" into your church; instead, ensure that your church is pursuing the future it is called to. The mindset I want you to hold on to is a mixture of a futurist mindset and design modality.

Futurist Mindset

Here are some challenges: Be curious, not judgemental. This simple retooling can help you rethink your beliefs and practices when faced with new evidence or feedback. Instead of being defensive or resistant to change, you can embrace the opportunity to improve and grow. It can help you change your mind when you realize that you were wrong or that there is a better option. Instead of being stubborn or prideful, you could admit your mistakes and learn from them. It can help you enjoy being wrong because it means discovering something new or surprising. Instead of being embarrassed or frustrated, you can celebrate your curiosity and willingness to experiment. Nurturing a culture of curiosity over judgment is essential for sustaining emerging technologies and disruptions.

Design it! Dream it! Do it!

Now, let's get practical. I am a design thinker at heart. To avoid jumping too far into the weeds, I want to apply design thinking. I use an aspect of design thinking called *Gamification* in my work. You can read about that in my other book :) *Let's Play Church.* In the context of a futurist mindset, design thinking offers a practical approach to navigating future uncertainties. It encourages us to set aside our preconceptions and deeply understand the problem. This approach fosters innovation and allows us to explore various possible solutions, iterate extensively through prototyping and testing, and implement through the customary deployment mechanisms.

What is it?

Design thinking is a non-linear, iterative process teams use to understand users, challenge assumptions, redefine problems, and create innovative solutions to prototype and test. It is most beneficial to tackle ill-defined or unknown problems.[11] The approach has been around for decades, but it only started gaining traction outside the design community after the 2008 Harvard Business Review article, *Design Thinking* by Tim Brown, CEO and president of IDEO.[12] By adopting design thinking, we can approach the future with an open mind, ready to learn from new experiences and adapt to emerging trends and technologies because it is a human-centered design, a thinking process built around the consumer with a leader assisting in discerning decisions. Design helps people apply creativity to solve real-world problems better than they otherwise would effectively. Design thinking equips us with

---

[11] Interaction Design Foundation. (2024). Design Thinking. Retrieved from https://www.interaction-design.org/literature/topics/design-thinking

[12] MIT Sloan School of Management. (2017, September 14). Design Thinking Explained. Retrieved from https://mitsloan.mit.edu/ideas-made-to-matter/design-thinking-explained

the tools to be proactive creators of the future rather than passive observers.

When I use design thinking I use a five question approach: What is, What if, What Wows, What works, similar to the general process of design: *Empathize, define, imagine, prototype, and test.* Let's continue with the design thinking process in the context of a church:

What is?

The "What is?" phase is about understanding the current reality. It's the foundation of the design thinking process. With a clear understanding of the current situation, it's possible to identify opportunities for improvement or innovation. In this phase, you're observing the surface and digging deeper to understand the underlying mechanisms and structures.

Identify the opportunity: What needs of your congregation and community can the church meet? (1 Corinthians 12:7)

What is the spoke of our work? What is the central mission or purpose that all our activities revolve around? (Matthew 28:19-20)

What are our non-negotiable values? What are the core beliefs and principles that guide our decisions and actions? (Colossians 3:23)

Make plans (Write the vision and make it plain): What are our goals, and how do we plan to achieve them? (Habakkuk 2:2)

Do your research: What do the scriptures and any relevant data or studies say about our mission and plans? (Proverbs 18:15)

Identify insights: What have we learned from our research that can inform our decisions and actions? (Proverbs 2:6)

After completing the "What is?" phase, you should comprehensively understand the current situation. This understanding will guide the rest of the design thinking process, ensuring that your efforts are grounded in reality and aimed at real, relevant challenges and opportunities.

What if?

The "What if?" phase is about imagining the possibilities. It's a chance to think beyond reality and envision a better future. This phase is crucial for innovation because it allows you to break free from existing constraints and explore new ideas.

> **Establish a bigger vision than usual:** What could we achieve if we trusted God to do more than we ask or imagine immeasurably? (Ephesians 3:20)
>
> **Brainstorm ideas:** What creative ways could we fulfill our mission and serve our community? (1 Corinthians 2:9)
>
> **Develop conceptual possibilities:** What might these ideas look like in practice? (Proverbs 16:3)

After the "What if?" phase, you should have a range of potential solutions to explore, these ideas represent different paths towards a better future, and the subsequent stages of the design thinking process will help you determine which path is the most promising.

What Wows?

The "What Wows?" phase identifies the most promising ideas from the "What if?" phase. It's a chance to narrow your options and focus on the most potential ideas to wow your users. This phase is crucial for ensuring that your efforts are focused and effective.

Acknowledge your assumptions: What assumptions are we making, and are they consistent with Scripture and reality? (Proverbs 3:5-6)

Prototype: How can we test our ideas to see if they are feasible and practical? (James 1:22)

What is different? How does our church stand out from others in a way that glorifies God and serves people? (1 Peter 2:9)

What has no other church ever done? What unique opportunities has God given us to serve Him and others? (1 Corinthians 12:4-6)

After the "What Wows?" phase, you should have a shortlist of high-potential ideas to move forward with. These ideas are your best bets for creating a wow experience for your users.

What Works?

The "What Works?" phase tests your ideas to see if they work. It's a chance to learn from real-world feedback and make necessary adjustments before fully implementing your solution. This phase is crucial for ensuring that your solution is effective and meets the needs of your users.

Get feedback: What do people think of our ideas and prototypes? (Proverbs 15:22)

Prototype again: How can we improve our ideas based on the feedback we received? (Proverbs 24:16)

Launch: How can we implement our ideas in a way that is faithful to our mission and beneficial to our community? (James 2:26)

Design an onramp for others: How can we involve more people in our mission and activities? (Hebrews 10:24-25)

After the "What Works?" phase, you should have a tested and refined solution ready for implementation. This solution represents your answer to the challenges and opportunities identified in the "What is?" phase, shaped by the possibilities explored in the "What if?" phase and validated through the "What Wows?" and "What Works?" phases. It's a testament to the power of design thinking and its ability to drive innovation and improvement.

Design thinking is a powerful tool for anyone looking to adopt a futurist mindset. It encourages curiosity, fosters empathy, and promotes a culture of innovation and adaptability. By embracing design thinking, we can better prepare for and actively shape the future. This mindset encourages continuous learning and adaptation, crucial to navigating this new media age.

Stages of Adoption

I'm sure you're asking what does this have to do with AI? I have shared a mindset essential for AI and a way for you to navigate change using Design theory. Now, let me temper your expectations. I have worked in churches all of my life as both a volunteer and paid leader. Here is what I have learned. The reason the Titanic sank was because it tried to turn too fast. Ships do not turn overnight; they take time.

James Everett's adoption theory is also known as the diffusion of innovations theory. This framework explains how new ideas and technologies spread. The theory, developed by Everett Rogers, identifies five key attributes that affect the adoption rate: relative advantage, compatibility, complexity, trialability, and observability. [13] These influence the adoption of innovation. Everett then categorizes adopters into five groups: innovators, early adopters, early majority, late majority, and laggards.[14]

---

[13] https://www.enablersofchange.com.au/what-are-the-factors-that-affect-adoption/
[14] https://theboldbusinessexpert.com/2020/11/02/diffusion-of-innovation-getting-past-the-first-wave-of-innovators-and-early-adopters-to-reach-the-tipping-point/

The theory has been widely used in various fields to understand people and predict the adoption of new practices and technologies. According to Everett, here are the percentages of each group:[15]

1.   Innovators (2.5%)

2.   Early Adopters (13.5%)

3.   Early Majority (34%)

4.   Late Adopters (34%)

5.   Laggards (16%)

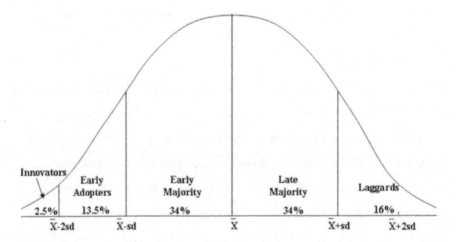

Figure 2.2. Adopter Categorization on the Basis of Innovativeness (Source: *Diffusion of Innovations, fifth edition* by Everett M. Rogers. Copyright (c) 2003 by The Free Press. Reprinted with permission of the Free Press: A Division of Simon & Schuster.)

Along with design thinking, this theory is so significant to our discussion. As you think about applying Artificial Intelligence, or as you consider where you are. Everett's Theory helps explain why an idea takes a while to take root. As you think about infusing AI, experimentation, and learning, know this: shifting a culture takes time and must build on the healthy, pre-existing parts

---

15

https://www.researchgate.net/publication/284675572_Detailed_review_of_Rogers'_diffusion_of_innovations_theory_and_educational_technology-related_studies_based_on_Rogers'_theory of the church culture. I wish I had remembered this earlier in my pastorate because it would've kept me from getting and staying in my feelings when my ideas initially did not get much traction. Also, it would have helped me motivate my members to adopt actionable steps sooner.

Let me tell you this.

Your church as a whole is not ready.
You may need more time to be ready.
As you roll it out, you will experience resistance.

And that's ok. That's why I'm here. I want you to see where you are, not forget where God is taking you, and be ready for the future.

"Preparation makes the difference."

"Cultivating curiosity fosters openness to exploration, innovation, and adaptation."

"Shifting a culture takes time and must build on the healthy, pre-existing parts of the church culture."

quotes to remember

questions to ask

How can we balance the preservation of tradition with the embrace of disruptive technologies in our church community?

What steps can we take to foster a culture of curiosity and openness to change within our congregation?

What challenges have you avoided in your church? Embrace it! By embracing the challenge, you embrace the change.

thing to try

7. ETHICS AND AI

One of the questions I get regularly about AI is Ethics. Whether we are looking at the ethical use of AI or the ethical implementation of AI, it's always there. In the first section, I stated that the entirety of our discussion theologically raised the conversation of morality and ethical engagement with A.I. Long story short, we are not ever going to escape a conversation on Ethics and AI, just as we have not run a discussion on ethics and every other area of life.

Ethics are essential to any field, as they help us navigate the complex moral issues that arise in our lives. The way that we as humans can think and reason together is through solid communication ethics. While technology enriches our world through increasing work output, communication, working from home, and more, it simultaneously challenges us to consider our moral and ethical foundations as we use them. Remember, humans are building this, using it, and are in control. **If AI is unethical, it's because of how we use it.** Before I get back into AI, I want to talk explicitly about Ethics.

What are Ethics?

Ethics, also called moral philosophy, is the division of philosophy concerned with how a person should behave in a matter considered morally correct or reasonable. Ethics are not just about following rules or doing the right thing; they are about making informed, thoughtful decisions that respect the dignity and well-being of all individuals involved. Ethical decision-making requires empathy, critical thinking, and a commitment to doing what is fair, just, and compassionate. Ethics means trying to figure out why one should behave morally and understanding the motivating factors for that behavior. The goal of ethics is to help define:

- o Good and Evil
- o Right and Wrong
- o Virtue and Vice
- o Justice and Crime.

It attempts to answer questions such as:

- o Is that sense of good or bad something naturally inside us, or is that sense placed there by a divine being?
- o Do we follow a moral code?

Ethics refers to principles or values guiding an individual's or a group's behavior, decision-making, and actions. Ethics can be related to various aspects of life, such as personal conduct, professional conduct, social norms, cultural beliefs, and legal codes. Ethics is the missing step between addressing the infiniteness of the universe and reconciling it with the daily existence of life on earth. If philosophy encourages moral behavior by asking the big "why" questions, then ethics is an exploration of that ethical behavior, and it seeks to formulate concrete "what" and "how" answers to the questions that philosophy poses.

What reasonable answer, or at least very informed or deeply held opinions, about the nature of the universe and the meaning of life if you don't know how to apply those "truths" to how you live your day-to-day life and interact with the world around you? Ethics seeks to determine how and why one should behave most virtuously. At its most elemental, ethics is about doing the right thing; the philosophy behind it is about deciding what those right things are. Those right things solidify our virtues, which are central to any discussion about ethics.

What are Virtues?

Moral philosophy is very much invested in determining not only the way humans ought to act but also the way they act. Ethics lead to quantifiable values, which are the few qualities that direct good behavior. Almost every different viewpoint on ethics is concerned with virtues because virtues have no ties to a specific religion or ethical ideology. And many are universal. (Some aren't, but that's a question for ethicists to debate.)

Virtues are moral excellences or qualities an individual possesses and uses to guide their thoughts, feelings, and actions. They are good traits or characteristics a person cultivates and practices to live a good and moral life. Virtues are often considered the foundation of ethical behavior and are valued in many cultures and societies. Many different virtues are recognized and respected across cultures and historical periods. Here are some examples of virtues:

- Honesty: the quality of being truthful and straightforward in one's actions and words.

- Courage is the bravery and willingness to take risks, especially in the face of danger or uncertainty.

- Compassion is the quality of feeling sorry for or empathizing with others, especially those suffering or in need.

- Fairness: the quality of being impartial and treating others fairly and equitably.

- Integrity: the quality of being honest, moral, and ethical in one's actions and beliefs.

- Respect: the quality of having a high regard for the rights, beliefs, and feelings of others.

- Perseverance: the quality of persisting in a task or pursuit despite obstacles or setbacks.

- Generosity: the quality of giving time, money, or other resources to help others or to good causes.

- Humility: the quality of being modest or unpretentious and recognizing one's limitations and mistakes.

- Self-control: the quality of being able to control one's emotions, desires, and actions, especially in difficult situations.

Virtues are often considered a combination of moral and emotional qualities associated with positive character traits, such as kindness, compassion, and empathy. Developing virtues is necessary for leading a good and fulfilling life and contributing to society's greater good. The foundation for this virtue-based ethical thought comes from the three pillars of ethics: Socrates, Plato, and Aristotle.

Ethics and the Ancient Greek Philosophers

Many philosophers wrote and taught in ancient Greece. But this golden era of Greek philosophy is dominated by three of the most famous and influential thinkers in Western history: Socrates, Plato, and Aristotle.

Socrates (ca. 470–399 BC) created much of the framework and methodology for approaching philosophy and ethics. Among these innovations is the "Socratic method." This method is a form of discourse and discussion based entirely on two or more parties asking each other an endless array of questions. The goal is to find common ground and highlight flaws in their arguments to get closer to some truth. Socrates thought that this ability separated humans from the rest of the animal kingdom, for we're the only animals capable of logic and reason.

Plato (ca. 428–348 B.C.).In Athens, Plato formed the first higher learning institution in the West, the Academy. One of his significant contributions to moral philosophy is the theory of forms, which explores how humans can live a life of happiness in an ever-changing, material world. Plato believed in the existence of an objective reality beyond our physical world. He thought pursuing knowledge and understanding of the Forms would lead to a just society. Plato also believed that individuals should balance reason, spirit, and desire.

The third pillar of ancient Greek philosophy is Aristotle (384–322 BC), a student of Plato's at the Academy and later a professor at the same institution. One of his primary theories deals with universals. He proposed whether there were "universals" and what they might be. This remains a significant focus of ethical inquiry today. Aristotle believed in finding the mean between extremes. He believed that virtue is achieved by practicing good habits and that living a virtuous life leads to happiness. Aristotle also believed that ethics should be based on practical reasoning and that moral virtues are developed through experience.

Ethics historically and currently lead to us engaging with the sheer impact of ethics with Artificial Intelligence. Long story short, it's complex. I suggest developing an AI policy and a list of procedures to govern and create boundaries on your Church's use of AI, which we will discuss in the next section.

Q what do I **take away?**

"If AI is unethical, it's because of how we use it."

"Virtues are moral excellences or qualities an individual possesses and uses to guide their thoughts, feelings, and actions."

"Ethics historically and currently lead us to engage with the sheer impact of ethics with Artificial Intelligence. It's complex."

How can your church integrate ethical considerations into their adoption and implementation of AI technologies to ensure they align with their values and principles?

What role do virtues play in shaping ethical behavior and decision-making within your church?

Concretize your values at your church. Those values and virtues will make decisions for you.

8: AI POLICY, LAWS, AND PROTECTION

Significant technological shifts always trigger a period of explosive growth where the technology and what's possible changes incredibly quickly; we're in that stage right now with AI systems; everyone is curious, scared, and interested in A.I. ChatGPT accumulated 100 million users in two months, which is faster than many other major apps. The future workforce uses AI, and bans will not be effective; over 40% of university students use ChatGPT for coursework, and 39% of prospective students say they wouldn't consider attending a college that ChatGPT and other LLMs. [16]Each month regularly brings new opportunities and surprises, many of which we can't anticipate, and require organizations to adapt quickly. Things are changing in big and

---

[16] The Guardian. (2023, February 2). ChatGPT surpasses 100 million users as OpenAI's fastest-growing app. The Guardian. https://www.theguardian.com/technology/2023/feb/02/chatgpt-100-million-users-open-ai-fastest-growing-app

small ways, making new capabilities feasible while also bringing new and unique concerns to light.

Time to Reach 100M Users

17

However, adopting this new technology at the right time and in a way that minimizes mistakes and bad outcomes can make great things happen for your organization. It's like catching the tail of a rocket ship just being launched but catching it in a way that doesn't burn you to a crisp. 30 or so years ago, we had a similar technological shift with the advent of the Internet. At the time, using the Internet for common everyday tasks was a big deal, and there was fear about how it would change how we worked. Now, we have accepted the Internet as a way of life, and it's an everyday experience to look things up on Google or shop online. In 30 years, AI systems will be the same; churches will use AI, making them more effective. AI policies can balance use with safety and security measures.

---

[17] Economy App. (2024, February 19). "ChatGPT reached 100M users in 2 months."In 20 years following the internet space, we cannot recall a faster ramp in a consumer internet app." ~ UBS" X. https://twitter.com/EconomyApp/status/1622029832099082241?ref=assemblyai.com

New technology adoption is scary

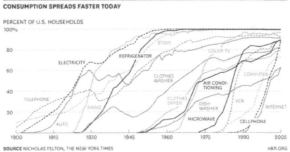

Caution is advisable; all out bans are not practical
https://medium.com/pronouncedkyle/new-technology-is-always-scary-8bf977a13773 CC-by hutchdatascience.org

18

Let's Build an AI Policy for Your Church

Let's talk about what elements an AI policy might have. (p.s. My thoughts and ideas will not be substituted for legal or ethical advice. They are only meant to give you a starting point for gathering information about AI policy and regulations to consider.) A good AI policy should be a living document that evolves as your Church adapts to AI use. As AI tools advance, so should the policy surrounding them. It should provide clear guidance and frameworks for developing, deploying, and using AI systems responsibly and ethically. Having a policy in the plan can provide extra security for your Church, staff, and attendees.

So, what is involved in a good AI policy document? A policy might discuss the following topics.

Purpose and scope: in this section, you might define your Church's goals and plans for AI use and what types of AI systems the policy will cover. This section also contains definitions of specific terms like what your

---

18 Kyle, P. (2021, September, 19). New technology is always scary. Medium.
https://medium.com/pronouncedkyle/new-technology-is-always-scary-8bf977a13773

organization considers AI or generative AI. The Purpose and Scope section can ensure everyone is aligned and avoid ambiguity.

Values and principles: this section states how your Church's core values and principles will guide your use and development of AI tools. Some possible principles might be fairness, transparency, accountability, safety, or privacy.

Governance and oversight. You should establish a clear governance strategy for overseeing AI initiatives. This includes the roles of those involved in decision-making and their responsibilities.

Data management and privacy: this section outlines data governance practices that ensure data quality, security, and responsible use in AI systems. Make sure your guidelines are compliant with relevant data privacy regulations.

Fairness and nondiscrimination: In this section, you can lay out how you might monitor and audit AI systems. This section can also include guidelines for developing or deploying AI to avoid perpetuating or exacerbating bias for discrimination based on protected characteristics, risk management, safety, and oversight. A section like this might lay out robust testing procedures to monitor, identify, and mitigate potential risks associated with AI systems, including security vulnerabilities, safety hazards, and unintended consequences. It can also identify ways to ensure oversight and accountability for AI systems, ensuring humans remain ultimately responsible for AI-driven decisions.

Education and training: This section describes how your church will provide training and education programs on AI systems and responsible AI development, deployment, and use.

Feedback and review: in this section, you can establish a mechanism for regularly reviewing and updating the AI policy as technology and best practices evolve. You may also want to implement procedures for members to give feedback about AI issues or concerns.

How you create an AI policy and what you cover in it will be highly dependent on what your Church's needs are. Unfortunately, there is no one-size-fits-all approach to AI policies, governance, and training. However, based on my experiences creating and implementing AI in the Church, I can offer some considerations. It is not enough to only build an AI policy. Building an AI support system that makes it possible for the people in your organization to adopt AI in safe and ethical ways is also important.

Thinking about your AI policy as just the beginning, not the entire thing, can be a way to protect you, your employees, and the people you serve. AI systems are being integrated into every aspect of our lives. Sometimes, these tools are self-explanatory, such as when an AI tool is applied to your data for predictive work. Other times, they could be more obvious, such as when integrated into standard desktop software such as copilots or auto-fill. It would help if you likely had a lot of different people with different perspectives to weigh in to get even close to what you want.

In terms of a comprehensive AI policy. Limiting policy and governance plan creation to just the chief data officer's office, the IT department, or the legal department might make things faster. However, the trade-off is that you are likely only covering a fraction of what you need. At a minimum, most Churches need representatives from legal compliance and governance. The speed at which AI technology changes is vast enough that creating applicable guidelines around its use is problematic. AI policy requires you to get diverse opinions and make them cohesive and coherent, which takes time.

The last thing you want to do is create a policy that no longer applies in three months when AI systems have changed again. Many people may need to solidify the answers to all questions, but the right people can help you find the answer. Training people to loop in the proper people and ask for help from the beginning might save them stress later.

AI Regulations

As generative AI continues to evolve and find new applications in various fields, from medicine to law, regulations are also rapidly developing. In the United States, AI regulation is still in its early stages, and there needs to be comprehensive federal legislation dedicated solely to AI regulation.[19] However, existing laws and regulations touch upon certain aspects of AI, such as privacy, security, and anti-discrimination. While the European Union has reached a landmark provisional deal on AI regulation with the EU AI Act, it's important to note that this act applies to AI regulation and use within the 27-member EU bloc and foreign companies operating within the EU. The EU AI Act could serve as a model for AI laws around the globe, including in the United States.[20] In the US, federal and state focus on regulating AI has begun. Many US states are beginning to form councils and task forces to look into AI. At the national level, President Biden's 2023

---

[19] Goodwin Law. (2023, April 12). US Artificial Intelligence Regulations: Watch List for 2023. Goodwin Law. https://www.goodwinlaw.com/en/insights/publications/2023/04/04_12-us-artificial-intelligence-regulations

[20] International Association of Privacy Professionals (IAPP). (2023, November). **US federal AI governance: Laws, policies and strategies**. IAPP. https://iapp.org/resources/article/us-federal-ai-governance/

executive order on AI remains the most relevant guidance.[21] The goal of these regulations is similar to that of the EU AI Act: to regulate AI to limit its capacity to cause harm. As in the EU, US regulations may cover the use of AI in biometric surveillance, such as facial recognition, and guide rules for large language models. However, the specifics of US AI regulations may differ from those in the EU. For instance, the categorization of AI-based products into levels based on risk, the requirements for technical documentation and detailed summaries about training data, and the financial penalties for violations may be different.

It's also worth noting that some individual industries in the US have already begun adopting policies about generative AI and may have long-standing policies about using other forms of AI, like machine learning. Given the rapidly evolving landscape of AI regulation, consulting with legal counsel or experts within your organization about the AI regulations that apply to you is crucial. As AI continues to disrupt various sectors, staying informed and compliant with relevant laws will be vital to navigating this transformative technology.

In the United States, AI regulation is still in its early stages, and there needs to be comprehensive federal legislation dedicated solely to AI regulation. . However, existing laws and regulations touch upon certain aspects of AI, such as privacy, security, and anti-discrimination. Here are some examples:

---

[21] Thomson Reuters. (2024, February, 11). **Legalweek 2024: Current US AI regulation means adopting a strategic — and communicative — approach.** Thomson Reuters. https://www.thomsonreuters.com/en-us/posts/legal/legalweek-2024-ai-regulation/

Federal Trade Commission (FTC) Guidelines: The FTC has issued guidelines that apply to AI and algorithms, particularly regarding fairness, transparency, and privacy

Health Insurance Portability and Accountability Act (HIPAA): In the healthcare sector, AI applications must comply with HIPAA regulations when handling patient data.

Fair Credit Reporting Act (FCRA): In the financial sector, AI systems used for credit scoring must comply with FCRA regulations.

President Biden's 2023 Executive Order on AI: This executive order guides AI development and use, particularly in the context of federal agencies.

State Privacy Laws: Many US states have privacy laws that may extend to AI systems that process certain types of personal data.

It's important to note that AI regulation in the US will consist of figuring out how existing laws apply to AI technologies rather than passing and using new, AI-specific laws. As AI continues to evolve, it's crucial to stay informed about the latest legal developments and consult with legal counsel or experts about the AI regulations that apply to you.

What does that mean for churches?

Data Privacy and Security: Churches that use AI systems to handle the personal data of their members must ensure that these systems comply with relevant privacy laws. This includes securing consent for data collection and ensuring data is stored and processed securely.

Transparency: If churches use AI systems, such as chatbots for pastoral care or AI-powered translation tools, they may need to identify that AI powers these services. This can help maintain trust and transparency with their congregation.

Ethical Considerations: Churches must consider the ethical implications of using AI. This includes considering issues such as the potential for bias in AI systems, the impact of AI on jobs within the church community, and the appropriate use of AI in a religious context.

Reskilling and Upskilling: As AI becomes more prevalent, church staff may need to reskill or upskill to use and manage AI systems effectively. This could involve learning new technical skills or understanding how to integrate AI tools into their existing workflows.

Legal Consultation: Given the rapidly evolving landscape of AI regulation, churches should consult with legal counsel to understand the rules that apply to them. This can help ensure that they are using AI in a legally compliant way.

Community Engagement: Churches can play a role in educating their community about AI and its implications. This could involve hosting discussions or workshops on AI's ethical, social, and religious impact.

Remember, while AI can offer many benefits, it's essential to use it in a way that aligns with the values and mission of the Church. It's also crucial to stay informed about the latest developments in AI regulation to ensure that any use of AI is compliant with relevant laws and regulations.

Q what do I **take away?**

"A good AI policy should be a living document that evolves as your Church adapts to AI use."

"AI policies can balance their use with safety and security measures."

"While AI can offer many benefits, it's essential to use it in a way that aligns with the values and mission of the Church.

quotes to remember

questions to ask

What steps can you take to foster a culture of ethical AI use and responsible innovation within their organizations?

How can you churches engage with legal counsel and experts to navigate the complex landscape of AI regulation and compliance?

Draw your boundary line with a sharpie. Be intentional to develop an AI policy!

thing to try

9. IMPLEMENTING AN AI STRATEGY IN YOUR CHURCH

Alright! Are you Ready to put AI to work in your Church? I will suggest a three-step process to build an AI strategy for your Church, including what needs to be in place before somebody can implement AI. We will also look at the consequences of the AI transformation on the traditional church model and how AI affects the culture.

Implementation

Building an AI strategy with relies on two pillars. One, evaluate and decide if AI applies to your Church and would help solve problems and improve processes. And two, if the answer to the first statement is yes, then ensure that your Church has people in place to maximize the use of AI.

The keyword for this section is data. Data-driven churches change everything because you do not have to question whether or not you can or should do something; the data speaks. How do we move data forward? Digitalization! **Digitization is a move from analog to digital practices.** Examples are moving from handwriting to typing on a computer or from film to digital cameras. Moving to a higher level of complexity, we have digital automatization so that technology assists you to expedite processes like automatic form-filling functions and the like. Digital transformation is a more comprehensive change introduced in an organization when there is already a high level of digitization and digital automation. How do you do this? An effective AI digitization strategy is threefold: **process, data, and knowledge.**

Process

It is essential to think of the reasons and the degree of fit between the characteristics of your Church and the benefits and costs of AI implementation before rushing into it. **AI is not good in itself.** AI is a set of tools that needs a precise place and purpose in your Church to be truly beneficial. For example, AI can delegate decision-making to algorithms and thus free up more human time to dedicate to other more complex and visionary tasks. In addition, AI can help churches meet members in different ways. AI can solve problems and improve processes for small-staffed churches, but these must be adapted to your organization's specific context.

The first step to consider introducing AI technology in your workplace is to evaluate the existing processes and structures and see if AI can help solve problems or improve flows in your specific arena. Not all issues need an AI solution. For example, I was working with a church that wanted a chatbot to enhance web interaction with people visiting a website. In concept, it was awesome! However, when we considered the lack of consistency in communication and language without the chatbot, the chatbot would not have been monitored, and there was not enough data to make an automated chatbot for the Church. It was better for us to consider church text options and to optimize the webpage for email communication more than a chatbot. When we did, I optimized their website navigation and provided an FAQ with better links, a faster and simpler solution. So, no AI for AI's sake, but contextualized it to implement other technology.

That means the first step to engaging with AI in your Church is evaluating your current processes and systems. As much as I love AI, if your Church still uses programs and phone trees and does not have a social media page, AI may not be the next step we need to discuss. Please do not stop reading! Let this book be an encouragement to build your church's technology foundation. Implementing AI can start even with a single process that is to become automatized.

Here are some questions I want you to ask yourself about your Church's Processes and procedures:
1. How do Problems get solved in our Church?
2. What steps do we go through to deal with problems?
3. Are there clear rules that define our problem-solving process?

Here are some thoughts to consider for your Church:
- Conduct a thorough assessment of existing church processes to identify areas that could benefit from AI.

- Evaluate the applicability of AI in solving specific challenges within your church community.

- Determine if there is a clear purpose and goal for introducing AI into church operations.

- Contextualize AI solutions to align with the unique needs and characteristics of the church environment.

- Explore opportunities for Automation and improved decision-making in church processes through AI.

Practical Next Steps for Churches:

- Implement AI as a pilot project in a specific church process, starting with a well-defined and manageable area.

- Use chatbots to improve user interaction on the church website, but only if it aligns with user needs.

- Explore AI applications to optimize church website navigation and provide FAQs for better user engagement.

- Investigate AI tools that align with the Church's goals, such as data analytics for understanding member needs.

- Provide training for church staff on utilizing AI tools and systems effectively.

Apps for Implementation:

- **Chatbot Platforms:** Utilize platforms like ManyChat or Chatfuel to introduce chatbots to enhance user interaction on the church website.

- **Data Analytics Tools:** Consider tools like Tableau or Power BI for analyzing church data and gaining insights into member needs.

- **Process Automation Platforms:** Explore solutions like Zapier or Integromat for automating specific church processes through AI.

Data

Data is the new oil; It should be treated as a commodity that an organization seeks out, minds, transforms, and uses to generate value for itself and its customers. While the phrase is catchy and reflects the perception that data is the world's most valuable resource, it has its pitfalls. For one, unlike oil, data is an endless resource that can be easily shared, raising the question of data ownership and privacy. Is the data about me, mine? Or does it belong to the company that tracks my every move to collect it? Data is valuable because it comes from how we use it to help attain our goals. In other words, data needs to have a purpose. For any AI system to work, the availability of data is crucial. This is why digitalization is a precondition for implementing any digital technology. While digitization has become a relatively straightforward process, one question remains. Which data must be tracked, and how much must be retained for an AI system to work correctly? The answer to this question depends on the problem that needs to be solved and the culture of your Church.

For an effective AI strategy, Data is essential. It is the primary ingredient for success, whether problem-solving involves classifying documents, detecting giving patterns, or finding abnormal activities that signal security breaches. Proper mechanisms of data management and data governance should also match data collection. When deciding where to start with AI implementation, consider beginning with areas covered by the best data in your Church. Then, the algorithms can really show off their power, performance, service encouragement, and proof of the benefits of implementing AI.

Here are some questions to consider as it relates to data and your Church.

    a.   What data is available about the problems in your Church?

    b.   What historical data do you have access to, and in what condition is it to help you get better as a church

Next Steps:

- Evaluate existing data sources within your Church and categorize them based on quality and format.

- Assess the suitability of available data for AI implementation and prioritize areas with high-quality data.

- Consider the ethical implications of data collection, usage, and privacy within the church context.

- Explore opportunities for digitization and recordkeeping improvements to enhance data availability.

- Develop a data governance framework to ensure data security, integrity, and regulation compliance.

Practical Next Steps for Churches:

- Identify areas where AI implementation could enhance efficiency or service delivery within church operations.

- Begin with areas that have well-structured and high-quality data for initial AI experimentation and implementation.

- Explore AI applications like data analytics tools or chatbots to improve member engagement, event management, and resource allocation.

- Invest in training and capacity building for church staff to utilize AI technologies effectively.

- Monitor and evaluate the impact of AI implementation on church operations and member satisfaction.

Apps for Implementation:

- **Data Analytics Tools:** Utilize platforms like Tableau, Power BI, or Google Analytics to analyze church data and gain insights.

- **Chatbot Platforms:** Consider chatbot solutions like ManyChat or Chatfuel to improve member engagement and provide instant support.

- **Data Management Systems:** Implement systems like Salesforce or Church Management Software (ChMS) to streamline data collection, storage, and analysis within the church community.

Knowledge

Once you evaluate processes, know your data, the last step to implementing an AI strategy for your Church is knowledge. That is, to ensure the organizational structure of your Church is competent enough to sustain the strategy. That is, inspecting the existing work configuration to link the future AI systems with existing systems. The questions that will guide us here are:

1. What current activities are taking place that would enhance or hinder your ability to use AI techniques to solve a specific problem?

2. What knowledge relevant to the implementation of AI technology exists?

AI technology is systemic; in other words, it benefits from large amounts of connected information. Awareness of the existing hierarchies of knowledge is imperative. Throughout this work, you continue to see that competence with disruption will assist with AI, not independent of each other. Knowing established hierarchies may result in resistance to the new technologies. To prevent this, I suggest charting the competence needs of the people in authority and addressing them head-on. Just like data, knowledge is a precious resource that needs to be fostered and rewarded. Here are some thoughts on questions to help discern an AI strategy:

Relevant Questions:

- What current activities in our organization could support or impede AI implementation?
- What knowledge relevant to AI exists within our organization, and where is it located?
- How does AI implementation align with existing and planned digital transformation initiatives?
- Are there criticisms or impending changes to current systems that could impact AI deployment?

Next Steps:

Conduct a thorough assessment of current processes and workflows to identify areas where AI could enhance efficiency or effectiveness.

- Evaluate existing knowledge and competencies related to AI techniques and capabilities.
- Consider the ethical implications of AI implementation and engage in discussions with stakeholders to address concerns.
- Explore AI-powered tools and applications that could streamline administrative tasks, improve communication with congregants, or enhance pastoral care.
- Invest in training programs or workshops to educate church leaders and volunteers about AI technologies and their potential applications.

- Implement pilot projects or small-scale initiatives to test the feasibility and impact of AI solutions in specific areas of church operations.

- Foster a culture of innovation and collaboration within the church community to encourage ongoing exploration and adoption of emerging technologies.

Suggested Apps for Implementation:

- **Church Management Software:** Apps like Planning Center, ChurchTrac, or Breeze offer features for scheduling, volunteer management, and communication.

- **Natural Language Processing Tools:** Applications that analyze and understand written or spoken language can assist in sermon preparation, counseling sessions, or community outreach efforts.

- **Data Analytics Platforms:** Platforms like Tableau or Power BI can help churches analyze attendance trends, track giving patterns, and make data-driven decisions for ministry planning.

Q what do I **take away?**

3

"AI is not good in itself. AI is a set of tools that needs a precise place and purpose in your Church to be truly beneficial."

"Introducing processes in one area of your business should be done while keeping in mind the fit with other ongoing or planned digital automation and transformation processes."

"Just like data, knowledge is a precious resource that needs to be fostered and rewarded."

How can your church ensure that AI implementation aligns with your unique organizational goals and values while addressing potential ethical concerns?

What strategies can your church employ to foster a culture of innovation and collaboration that supports ongoing exploration and adoption of emerging technologies like AI?

Be deliberate in making a decision on integrating AI into your church operations by carefully evaluating, aligning, and nurturing the knowledge and skills necessary for its effective implementation.

10. AI AND JOB REPLACEMENT

I have Pastored for a long time now, and I understand that a majority of our members are on hourly jobs that are technical. Often a question I receive when I teach on AI and Church is concern from other Pastors worried about their members jobs and whether or not those jobs will be replaced. Simultaneously, that concern is about the bottom line at our individual churches as well. **Will AI Replace Jobs?** Yes and no. I am a huge proponent of the idea that artificial intelligence will not replace people. Instead, it will replace people who do not use Artificial Intelligence. AI affects different jobs in different ways. Many of your members may need more time to engage with AI, so I will use this chapter to engage with the disruption to the workforce they may experience. Huang & Rust proposed a theory of AI job replacement where AI will first take over mechanical tasks, then analytical, then intuitive, and most likely even empathetic tasks.

Huang and Rust's theory of job replacement by AI argues for a progression of AI task replacement from lower to higher intelligence.[22] The first stage occurs when AI takes over mechanical tasks and analytical, intuitive, and empathetic functions within a specific job. The final fifth stage is replacing the human worker with the AI algorithm with a human moving to other arenas. Note that these stages are within the same job and that for most of these stages, the human and the AI work side by side, with the machine assisting the human. Stage five has yet to be fully reached.

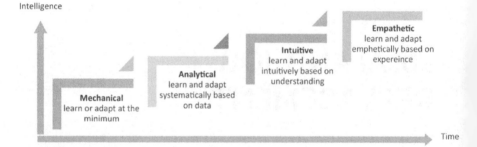

Mechanical intelligence concerns the ability to perform routine repeated tasks automatically. Little creativity is involved since the functions are similar and have been internalized without requiring too much new thinking. Examples of professions that rely heavily on mechanical intelligence are call center agents, retail salespersons, waiters and waitresses, and taxi drivers. Once upon a time, some humans were employed to perform complicated mathematical calculations. Much of the current AI

---

[22] A theory of job transformation - Huang, M. H., & Rust, R. T. (2018). Artificial intelligence in service. Journal of Service Research, 21(2), 155-172.

applications are in analytical intelligence, where computers have become equal to, if not better than, humans since they are faster and have better memory and recall capacities than human brains.

Intuitive intelligence is the ability to think creatively and adjust effectively to noble situations, creative and holistic tasks based on experience and context, knowledge required, and intuitive intelligence. Some professions that rely heavily on intuitive intelligence are management consultants, lawyers, doctors, sales managers, and senior travel agents. These professionals can see the big picture and make sense of the results of the data analysis. So far, humans are better than machines at performing these tasks.

Empathetic intelligence is the ability to recognize and understand other people's emotions, respond appropriately, and influence others' emotions. Any profession that requires people skills such as relationship building, leadership, advocating, and negotiation uses empathetic intelligence. Some examples are pastors, flight attendants, frontline workers, psychologists, psychiatrists, politicians, and negotiators. Empathetic AI based on practical computing would be a machine that would behave like it would feel. This area is where humans have, by far, the upper hand. Even if AI has been increasingly used in psychological therapy, some mechanical intelligence requires one to learn or adapt at a minimum.

Analytical intelligence learns and adapts systematically based on data. Intuitive intelligence learns and adapts intuitively based on understanding. Empathetic intelligence learns and adapts empathetically based on experience.

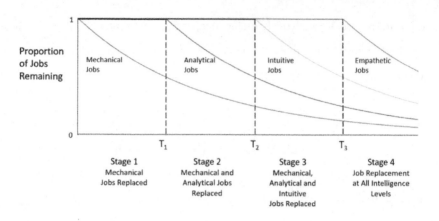

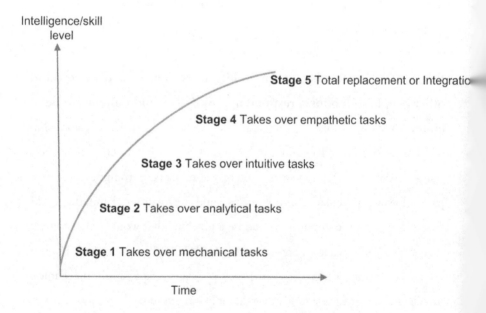

While we have yet to reach that place, we are peeking into what is possible, the opportunity to sketch out possible AI scenarios.

Theories of Job Replacement

Option 1: Human Interaction as a Premium Alternative: Human interaction will become the premium alternative when most jobs become automated. For some services, customers may want to pay extra for having contact with a human representative. So, AI and people will be employed simultaneously for the same job but with different price tags.

Option 2: Complementary Division of Labor: Humans and machines have a complementary division of labor, even under the scenario in which AI can develop empathy. Many argue that computers will not be able to replicate human emotions fully but that they will feel logical. So, humans who would continue to think holistically would be supported by AI systems and become even more potent in this way.

Option 3: Human-Centric View of AI.: This option is based on a human-centric view of AI, where people retain complete control over AI development. Machines will be allowed to take over those industry's jobs or tasks that no human wants to engage with. People can choose to work in those jobs that give them a sense of satisfaction or fulfillment, or as an alternative, the machines would work with humans, having nothing else to do but enjoy their lives.

Option 4: Physical and Cognitive Integration of Humans and Machines: This scenario proposes a physical and cognitive integration of humans and machines. In this scenario, people can have body and mind enhancements, or what Elon Musk calls a merger between biological and digital intelligence. Musk is currently pursuing the Neuralink project in which a neural implant will let one control a computer or mobile device by the power of their thought.

Option 5: Machines Completely Dominate Over Humans: The fifth and most pessimistic scenario is when machines completely dominate over humans.

Option 6: AI Augmentation: In this scenario, AI is used to augment human capabilities rather than replace them. AI tools are used to enhance human decision-making, creativity, and productivity.

Option 7: AI as a Tool: AI is viewed as a tool that humans use to perform tasks more efficiently and effectively. This scenario focuses on using AI to automate routine tasks, freeing humans to focus on more complex and creative tasks.

Option 8: AI and Humans Co-evolving: In this scenario, humans and AI co-evolve. As AI capabilities advance, humans adapt and evolve, learning new skills and ways of working with AI.

Option 9: AI as a Collaborator: In this scenario, AI is viewed as a collaborator rather than a human replacement. AI and humans work together, each bringing their unique strengths.

All these scenarios are futuristic. But if Huang and Rust's theory is correct, there is a concrete lesson for the here and now. Intuition and empathy, soft skills, and relational and people skills will likely be the last replaced by an AI system. So, the necessity to educate and train our people will build competence for the long term.

AI-driven transformation has the potential to disrupt competence hierarchies within organizations. The best way to navigate this disruption is through creative accumulation, where old knowledge is preserved while new knowledge is added creatively. Hence, why I have been harping so much on optimist and futurist thinking where you, as a Pastor and leader, must evolve from being past-oriented and evaluative to being more future-oriented and prescriptive, yes, these strategies may be met with resistance as they threaten static identity. So what? Now, let's dive into ways we, as churches, can engage this AI and leverage it for the better.

Competence

The Church is non-disruptable. I want to make that very clear. Jesus Christ is the same yesterday, today, and forever (Hebrews 13:8). Sin cannot ruin God's Church unless we let it. Jesus and the goals of God's Church will always stand on Matthew 28 to spread the Gospel. That will never be disrupted. Jesus does not change, but our culture and the people a part of it do. I genuinely believe that in the realm of church management and community engagement, disruption is necessary. Our need for organization, engagement, adherence to paper, and the like needs a disruption. Thus far, I have explained the importance of disruption using AI as a tool. One effective strategy to navigate this is human-centered design; my favorite is gamification. This concept incentivizes engagement and participation through game-like elements. (If you want a more extended exposition on Gamification, Read my Book, *Let's Play #Church.*) Since we see AI's continual growth, I want to assist you in exploring how gamification can facilitate adaptation and foster a culture of learning within religious organizations.

Learning organizations grow.

I'm sure there are relics in your Church that you inherited or brought that are no longer relevant. I am not saying to get rid of relics and replace them with AI; I am challenging you to ask questions about them. **The good old days are gone,** so let's disrupt by asking questions of relevance and engaging in what I call *Creative Accumulation.* Creative accumulation preserves traditional knowledge while integrating innovative approaches. Consider an auditing firm where technology has revolutionized past-oriented roles into future-oriented and authoritarian ones. Churches can maintain relevance amidst disruption by embracing technology while upholding core principles.

Here are some Creative Accumulation possibilities:

- **Time Capsule of Church Memories:** Encourage congregation members to contribute items or messages reflecting their experiences and aspirations within the Church, to be sealed in a time capsule and opened at a future anniversary or milestone event.
- **Innovative Worship Experiences:** Explore interactive worship formats incorporating multimedia elements, virtual reality simulations, or participatory storytelling techniques to deepen engagement and foster spiritual growth among attendees.
- **Faith-Based Hackathons:** Organize hackathons or innovation challenges where participants collaborate to address pressing community needs or explore creative solutions to contemporary theological questions, promoting collaboration and experimentation within the church community.

Reskilling and Upskilling

Two strategies are available for creative accumulation: **reskill or upskill.** Reskill means that one needs to diversify one's knowledge repertoire, learn new things, become familiar with new tech, and take on new roles. Upskill means to grow and improve one's existing knowledge about the same domain, to update, but primarily to stay in the same knowledge area. To reskill or upskill sounds appealing, as it implies learning new things and striving for positive development.

Why can resistance meet such strategies? Even if members are not at risk of losing their title or position in the Church or their job or income outside of the Church, re or upskilling may threaten their identity. Professional identity, like all group identities, is defined by exclusivity. The in-group members possess some qualities that differentiate them from others, the out-groups. A strong church leadership identity comes with being time-served or family-time-served. Someone whose last name has been in the same seat has authority. Reskilling or upskilling your Church with AI implies new organizational problems requiring unique solutions. Solutions they may not like.

Here's what I will tell you from experience: **Change or Die**. This is the imperative with Jonah in Jonah 4. Will we, as a church, sit under the juniper tree mad that our Anointing can change the entire trajectory of a community? We want the safety of a tree, so we ask God to preserve the tree. Or will we get up, return to Ninevah, and participate even if we lose the tree? Let the tree represent stable giving, old givers, and last names. Will you grow Ninevah, or will you love the tree?

New technology requires new experts who typically have to be brought from outside the Church and introduce new problems and solutions. AI disruption means that the old competence hierarchy is no longer valid. Ancient knowledge is considered less valuable compared to new knowledge. This may mean new Technology ministries. *Yes, let me be the bully.* Introducing AI systems damages the standing of static people and their reputation in the Church. So, their logical strategy is resistance. They are choosing death.

Stop here and think about your church organization and your competence needs. Do you want to retrain the existing people, or do you want to engage in something different? As technology reshapes competence hierarchies, existing employees may perceive their standing and reputation as jeopardized. However, you can mitigate resistance through strategic reskilling and upskilling programs. By nurturing a culture of continuous learning and providing tangible incentives, churches empower their workforce to embrace change and thrive in an evolving environment.

Next Steps for Pastors:

Establish Learning Communities: Create small groups or forums where members can share knowledge and skills, fostering a culture of mutual learning and support.

Offer Skill-building Workshops: Organize workshops or seminars on relevant topics such as digital literacy, pastoral counseling techniques, or community outreach strategies.

Implement Mentorship Programs: Pair seasoned members with newer ones to facilitate knowledge transfer and skill development.

Questions to Ask:

-How can we encourage active participation in reskilling and upskilling initiatives within our congregation?

-What skills or knowledge areas do our members need to develop to serve the church community better?

Addressing Competence Needs: Balancing Tradition and Innovation

Churches must assess competence needs to navigate disruption effectively. The decision to retrain existing staff or hire new personnel requires careful consideration of short-term requirements and long-term trends. For instance, proficiency in programming languages like R or Python may offer immediate benefits but necessitates evaluation of future relevance. By aligning competence development with organizational goals and technological advancements, churches can adapt proactively and remain resilient in the face of change.

Next Steps for Pastors:

Conduct Competency Assessments: Evaluate staff and volunteers' current skill sets and knowledge levels to identify areas for improvement or expansion.

Explore Cross-disciplinary Training: Encourage individuals to diversify their expertise by learning from different areas within the Church, fostering interdisciplinary collaboration.

Facilitate Knowledge Sharing Sessions: Organize regular meetings or conferences where members can exchange insights and best practices related to traditional and innovative church practices.

Questions to Ask:

-How can we balance preserving traditional practices and embracing innovative approaches within our church community?

-What emerging trends or technologies could enhance our ministry's effectiveness, and how can we prepare our team to adapt to these changes?

Cultivating a Culture of Learning

A culture of learning lies at the heart of successful adaptation in churches. By prioritizing employee development and investing in reskilling and upskilling initiatives, churches foster an environment conducive to growth and innovation. Gamification is the way to lead by incentivizing participation in training sessions and promoting engagement with new technologies. Through continuous reflection and support, churches empower individuals to embrace change and drive success in a non-stop, ever-evolving culture.

Next Steps for Pastors:

Integrate Learning into Worship Services: Incorporate educational components into sermons, Bible studies, or fellowship gatherings to encourage continuous spiritual and intellectual growth.

Recognize and Reward Learning Milestones: Celebrate individual and collective achievements in skill development and knowledge acquisition, reinforcing the value of lifelong learning.

Embrace Innovative Learning Tools: Explore interactive online platforms, mobile apps, or virtual reality experiences to engage members in immersive learning experiences tailored to their interests and preferences.

Questions to Ask:

-How can we foster a sense of curiosity and enthusiasm for learning among our congregation members of all ages?

-What role can technology play in enhancing our Church's educational programs and promoting continuous personal and professional development?

AI is here. It will disrupt culture and the world; we can lead disruption before disruption disrupts us. Adaptation in churches requires a multifaceted approach that integrates tradition with innovation. By leveraging gamification, addressing competence needs, and nurturing a learning culture, your Church can navigate disruption with resilience and foresight. As technology continues to reshape the local Church, embracing change becomes a necessity and an opportunity for growth and renewal. Through collective effort and commitment to lifelong learning, we got this!

Q what do I **take away?**

"Change or Die. This is the imperative with Jonah in Jonah 4. Will we, as a church, sit under the juniper tree mad that our Anointing can change the entire trajectory of a community?"

"Intuition and empathy, soft skills, and relational and people skills will likely be the last replaced by an AI system.

"The good old days are the gone old days."

quotes to **remember**

questions to ask

How can your church balance the preservation of traditional practices with the integration of innovative approaches in the face of AI disruption?

What role can technology play in enhancing educational programs and promoting continuous personal and professional development among members?

2

Engage with ways you can make your church a learning organization. If nothing else, embrace small change.

thing to **try**

11. ROBOTICS

Let's spend some time on Robotics. As we spend a moment on robotics and how AI drives this field forward, you will see many similarities with previous topics, such as autonomy. Thus, while we may not explicitly cover topics like ethical concerns in this chapter, the same worries and thoughts will emanate in your mind. Let's first start with definitions to ensure clarity on robotics.

What is robotics? Robotics is the field of study that involves the design, instruction, operation, and application of robots. Robots can perform tasks or functions without human intervention or supervision. These machines are built on methods or approaches that enable robots to perform tasks or functions effectively and efficiently. One of the standard robotic techniques is sensing. This refers to the ability of robots to perceive their environment using sensors such as cameras, microphones, lasers, and radars. Sensing enables robots to collect data or information that can be used for navigation recognition and localization.

AI can be integrated with all types of robots to help them accomplish various tasks. The three examples I want to engage with are Industrial, Service, and Social Robots.

Industrial robots. These robots perform tasks or functions in industrial settings such as manufacturing, assembly, or warehousing. Industrial robots use AI to improve their speed, accuracy, and flexibility and reduce human error and risk. For example, industrial robots can use computer vision to identify objects or defects, natural language processing to communicate with human workers, and machine learning to optimize their movements or processes. They are also used in various manufacturing, assembly, and warehousing sectors.

Here are some examples

- **ABB**: ABB's wide range of industrial robots can perform tasks like arc and spot welding, material handling functions like sorting and packaging, and quality control.
- **Comau**: Comau's industrial robots, which work in automotive, logistics, and other industries, can handle payloads ranging from 3 to 650 kilograms.
- **Denso Robotics**: Denso's industrial robots are being used by companies worldwide. Applications range from ultrasonic and laser welding to aerospace, semiconductors, and pharmaceuticals surface finishing.

Service robots: These are robots that perform tasks or functions in service settings such as healthcare, education, or entertainment. Service robots use AI to improve their interaction, personalization, adaption, and enhance human well-being and satisfaction. For example, service robots can use speech recognition to understand human commands or queries, emotion recognition to respond to human moods or feelings, and reinforcement learning to learn from human feedback or rewards. Here are some examples:

- **Roomba:** Roomba is a domestic service robot that performs tasks such as cleaning floors.
- **Milo by RoboKind:** Milo is a humanoid robot designed to interact with humans, especially children with autism.
- **Connie by Hilton:** Connie is a robot that assists in customer service in the hospitality industry

Social robots: These are robots that perform tasks or functions in social settings such as homes, offices, or public spaces. Social robots use AI to improve communication, collaboration, and empathy and foster human trust and acceptance. For example, social robots can use natural language generation to generate human-like speech or text, facial expression generation to display human-like emotions or expressions, and social learning to learn from human behavior or norms. Here are some examples:

- **Furhat by Furhat Robotics:** Furhat is a customizable social robot for prototype and application development.
- **Jibo:** Jibo was a personal home assistant robot.
- **Sophia by Hanson Robotics:** Sophia is a humanoid robot that uses AI to interact with humans.

What about the Church?

While we are still in the early stages of robotics, it will eventually get to our churches. Here are some opportunities I am projecting that robotics can be a part of our church experiences.

Assistance in Administrative Tasks:

Robots equipped with AI can assist in administrative tasks such as managing databases, scheduling events, and sending notifications to the Church. Advanced humanoid robots could greet visitors and provide directions on the church campus, enhancing the visitor experience.

Facilitating Accessibility and Inclusivity:

Robots can be programmed to provide real-time translations of sermons and events, ensuring that non-native speakers or individuals with hearing impairments can fully participate. Beyond the walls of the Church into the online Church, Tele-robots could allow remote worshippers, such as the elderly or those with mobility issues, to attend services virtually, engage in fellowship activities, and feel present at home.

Enhancing Worship Experiences:

Robots with multimedia capabilities can assist in presenting songs, scripture readings, and other visual aids during worship services. Also, if you make them interactive, they can lead prayers, recite scriptures, or even preach. Too far?

Supporting Outreach and Community Engagement:

Robots can accelerate community outreach engagement. Imagine a robot equipped with social media integration that can assist in disseminating information about church events, volunteer opportunities, and community outreach programs. Furthermore, if they are mobile robots, they can help with donation collection and roam around the church premises during fundraising events with immediate measurements and returns.

Providing Educational and Youth Programs:

Lastly, educational robots could be used in Sunday school classes or youth programs to facilitate interactive learning experiences, teach biblical lessons, and engage young participants. Beyond those classes, imagine robotics workshops and STEM programs hosted by the Church could introduce children to robotics technology, fostering interest in science, technology, engineering, and mathematics (STEM) disciplines within a faith-based context.

By no means are these exhaustive or even actual; instead, if we consider what is possible, I believe that robots can contribute to the activities and functions of local churches, ranging from practical administrative support to innovative approaches in worship, outreach, and community engagement. While some applications may already be feasible with existing technology, others represent forward-looking concepts that leverage the potential of robotics to enhance religious practices and foster spiritual growth within congregations.

Of course, AI and robotics bring forth several challenges and risks. They also offer advantages such as enhancing task quality and efficiency and reducing human error. They also drive productivity, innovation, and the creation of new opportunities. Moreover, they have the potential to improve human well-being and positively address societal and environmental issues. However, these advantages require careful attention to broader issues such as trust, acceptance, and moral and legal considerations. By understanding and effectively managing these challenges and risks, organizations can harness the transformative potential of AI and robotics while ensuring responsible and ethical implementation.

Q what do I **take away?**

quotes to **remember**

3

Robots can accelerate community outreach engagement."

"Advanced humanoid robots could greet visitors and provide directions on the church campus, enhancing the visitor experience."

"Leverage the potential of robotics to enhance religious practices and foster spiritual growth within congregations."

questions to **ask**

How might the integration of robotics and AI in your church challenge traditional notions of interaction and engagement?

What ethical considerations should churches and religious leaders prioritize when considering the implementation of robotics?

2

1   Prayer.

thing to **try**

12: ANSWERS TO QUESTIONS FROM PASTORS

I pray that you learned something reading this work and that it answered as many questions as possible regarding AI and the church. But, to ensure I covered as many bases as possible, I reached out to some pastor friends and asked them precisely what they would want in a book on AI. Here are some questions I may have yet to engage explicitly, but I wanted to make sure you had an answer!

1. **How do we help people past their fears from pop culture films (Terminator, Minority Report, iRobot, etc.)?**

Addressing fears about Artificial Intelligence, especially those influenced by pop culture and science fiction films, involves education, transparency, and open dialogue. Here are some strategies:

*   **Education**: One of the most effective ways to alleviate fears is through education. This involves explaining what AI is, how it works, and its real-world applications. It's important to clarify that AI is a tool created by humans to solve problems and improve efficiency, and it doesn't have consciousness or malicious intent.
*   **Transparency**: Being transparent about how AI is used, particularly regarding data privacy and security, can help build trust. This includes explaining how AI systems make decisions and the measures in place to ensure these systems are used ethically and responsibly.
*   **Open Dialogue**: Encourage open discussions about AI and its implications. This can involve hosting workshops or forums where people can express their concerns and ask questions.
*   **Real-world Examples**: Highlight real-world examples of how AI is being used for good, such as in healthcare for disease diagnosis, in education for personalized learning, and in environmental conservation for tracking and protecting wildlife.
*   **Regulation and Oversight**: Discuss the role of regulation and oversight in ensuring that AI is used ethically and responsibly. This can help reassure people that checks and balances are in place to prevent misuse of AI.
*   **Human in Control**: Emphasize that humans are in control of AI. AI is a tool we use, control, and operate within our set parameters.

Remember, it's natural for people to fear what they don't understand, and movies often dramatize AI for entertainment. We can help demystify AI and address these fears by providing accurate information and fostering open dialogue.

2. **How can we use AI to improve youth discipleship?**

It's essential to be cautious about using AI with children, particularly children aged 0-6, where development and interaction priorities lie outside the realm of technology. However, with responsible implementation, AI can offer valuable tools for youth discipleship across age groups. Here are some ideas, categorized by age range:

Age 0-6:

- **Focus on human connection, not AI**—nurture relationships with parents and caregivers who lead in faith formation. Explore sensory-rich activities and interactive storytelling with a faith-based theme.
- **Educational apps with parental oversight:** Consider apps like "Bible for Me" or "Read Along Bible Kids" for interactive Bible stories, but remember, these are supplements, not replacements for human interaction.
- **Practical Ways**
    - **Interactive Bible Stories**: Use AI to create interactive and engaging Bible stories that can help children understand and remember the teachings of the Bible.
    - **Personalized Learning**: AI can analyze each child's learning patterns and customize the content to suit their learning style.
- **Apps**
    - **Bible App for Kids**: Interactive animations, games, and activities to help kids learn about God.
    - **JellyTelly**: Provides safe and fun Christian videos for children.
- **AI Tools**
    - **ChatGPT**: Can create educational materials for Sunday school classes.
    - **DeepL Translator**: Useful for translating bible study materials into different languages.

- *Age 6-12:*
    - **Personalized learning tools:** Implement apps like "LightSail" or "AIO School" for personalized Bible study guides based on age and interests.
    - **Interactive Bible apps:** Engage kids with apps like "The Bible App for Kids" or "Olive Tree Bible for Kids" for interactive stories, quizzes, and games.

- o **AI-powered chatbots:** Use educational chatbots like "Cleverbot" or "Mitsuku" to answer basic questions about the Bible or faith in a safe, interactive way. Remember, these are not replacements for human mentors and should be used with guidance.
- o **Creative expression tools:** Encourage faith-based storytelling and music creation with apps like "Bible Doodle" or "Music Maker Jam."

- **Practical Ways**
  - o **AI Tutors:** Use AI tutors to provide personalized Bible study lessons.
  - o **Virtual Reality:** Use VR to create immersive Bible stories.
- **Apps**
  - o **Superbook Kids Bible App:** Offers engaging Bible games and activities.
  - o **Guardians of Ancora:** A game that allows kids to explore Bible stories.
- **AI Tools**
  - o **QuillBot:** This can help rewrite and improve the readability of Bible study materials for this age group.
  - o **Jasper AI:** Helps prepare entire content articles, blocks, or outlines in seconds

Age 13-18:

- **Community building and discussion:** Use platforms like "Discord" or "GroupMe" to create safe online spaces for youth groups and meetings. Encourage responsible online behavior and digital citizenship.
- **Mentorship and support:** Utilize AI chatbots like "Woebot" or "Koko" to offer anonymous emotional support and mental health resources. Remember, these are not replacements for professional counseling.
- **Content creation and outreach:** Leverage AI tools like "Canva" or "Wix" to create faith-based content like podcasts, videos, or websites for peer-to-peer outreach and engagement.
- **Bible study and reflection:** Explore apps like "Bible Gateway" or "YouVersion" for personalized Bible study plans and journaling prompts.

- **Social action and volunteerism:** Use platforms like "VolunteerMatch" or "Idealist" to connect youth with faith-based volunteer opportunities aligned with their passions.
- **Practical Ways**
  - **Online Bible Studies:** Use AI to facilitate online Bible studies, allowing youth to connect and learn together throughout the week.
  - **AI Chatbots:** Use AI chatbots for pastoral care and to answer questions about the Church's history and upcoming events
- **Apps**
  - **YouVersion Bible App:** Offers hundreds of Bible versions and a feature that allows users to compare different versions of the Bible2
- **Echo Prayer:** Allows teens to keep track of their prayers and pray for others.
- **AI Tools**
  - **ChatGPT:** Can be used to facilitate online bible studies
  - **Zoomscape.ai:** This makes it more accessible for churches to host and run successful online meetings, conferences, or Bible studies without physical spaces.

3. How can AI enhance without distracting from corporate worship?

Integrating AI into corporate worship is a delicate thought. I, too, want to balance the potential benefits of AI, preserve the essence of prayer, and avoid distractions. Here are some points to consider:

Possible benefits of AI:

- **Accessibility:** AI-powered chatbots and robots can answer basic questions about faith, scripture, or Church activities, aiding newcomers and those with specific needs.
- **Personalization:** AI can personalize prayer experiences, suggest relevant scripture passages, or curate devotional content based on individual preferences.

- **Engagement:** Interactive virtual tours of religious sites or augmented reality experiences can enhance understanding and engagement with sacred spaces.
- **Music and liturgy:** AI can assist with composing music, generating hymns, or translating prayers into different languages.
- **Accessibility:** Language translation tools can facilitate worship for diverse communities.

Potential distractions and concerns:

- **Depersonalization:** Overreliance on AI could create a sterile, impersonal worship experience lacking the depth of human connection.
- **Misinterpretation:** AI interpretation of religious texts or doctrines could lead to understanding and accurate information.
- **Technical difficulties:** Glitches or malfunctions during services could be disruptive and undermine the occasion's solemnity.
- **Overdependence:** Excessive reliance on AI could diminish individual reflection, critical thinking, and personal responsibility in faith journeys.
- **Ethical considerations:** AI raises ethical questions about data privacy, potential bias in algorithms, and the role of human leadership in religious communities.

Approaches to using AI responsibly:

- **Focus on enhancing, not replacing:** AI should support human leadership and interaction, not replace it.
- **Transparency and trust:** Explain how AI is used and ensure ethical data practices.
- **Community involvement:** Include diverse voices in decision-making about AI integration.
- **Prioritize human connection:** Encourage face-to-face interaction, shared experiences, and meaningful dialogue.
- **Focus on spiritual growth:** Ensure AI tools align with the community's core values and spiritual goals.

Remember, the future of AI in worship is a conversation, not a predetermined outcome. Carefully evaluate the potential benefits and drawbacks, involve your community in discussions, and prioritize the core values of your faith tradition. As with any technology, the key lies in using AI responsibly and thoughtfully to enhance, not replace, humans' unique connection with their faith.

4. How do we make AI accessible across generations while destigmatizing technology within black churches in a post-pandemic world?

Making AI accessible and destigmatizing technology within Black churches in a post-pandemic world requires the same thing that you, as a pastor, have used in other areas—honesty, bridge building, trust sustaining, and moving forward. What we make big is big; don't make it big!

First, start with **Addressing Concerns:**

- **Transparency and education:** Organize workshops and discussions to explain AI in simple terms, its potential benefits and risks, and how data privacy is protected. Highlight AI applications already used in daily life (e.g., language translation, online recommendations) to normalize the technology.
- **Focus on ethical uses:** Emphasize how AI can be used for social good, addressing issues like racial justice, healthcare access, and education equity. This resonates with the values often held by Black churches.
- **Address privacy concerns:** Clearly explain data collection practices and ensure robust data security measures are in place. Offer opt-out options for those uncomfortable with data use.
- **Bring in other voices:** Pastors like me, who know the AI world and can speak the language of Church and tech.

Bridging the Digital Divide:

- **Digital literacy training:** Offer workshops and resources to teach basic computer skills and how to use AI-powered tools safely and effectively—partner with local colleges, tech companies, or community organizations to provide support.
- **Affordable technology access:** Explore subsidized internet plans, community Wi-Fi hotspots, or shared device programs to ensure

technology isn't a barrier. Leverage existing church resources and partnerships to create accessible technology hubs.

- **Culturally relevant applications:** Develop or choose AI tools specifically designed for the needs of Black communities, incorporating culturally appropriate language, themes, and imagery. Partner with Black-owned tech companies or researchers to develop culturally sensitive solutions. (I created a

Build Trust:

- **Community involvement:** Include diverse voices from the congregation in discussions and decision-making about AI integration. This ensures solutions resonate with community needs and concerns.
- **Focus on human connection:** Emphasize how AI should complement, not replace, human interaction in the church community. AI tools should aid communication, connection, and spiritual growth, not diminish them.
- **Highlight success stories:** Showcase examples of how other Black churches have successfully used AI for positive outcomes. This can inspire trust and encourage wider adoption.
- **Start small and build momentum:** Begin with pilot projects using simple AI tools like educational apps or chatbots. As comfort and experience make, expand to more complex applications.

Additional Points:

- **Address systemic issues:** Acknowledge that the digital divide and technology apprehension often stem from historical and systemic factors. Work to address these root causes while providing immediate solutions.
- **Empower youth:** Engage young people in learning and using AI tools. Their enthusiasm and tech-savvy can bridge generational gaps and promote positive adoption.
- **Celebrate innovation:** Recognize and celebrate Black innovators and developers in the tech field. This fosters trust and showcases the potential for AI to empower Black communities.

5. How do I explain AI to my Church?

Explaining Artificial Intelligence (AI) to Church Leaders requires finding ways to communicate the concepts and implications of AI in a way that is relevant to their context and concerns. Here are a few approaches to consider:

- **Start with the basics:** Many church leaders may not be familiar with the technical details of AI, so it can be helpful to start with the basics. Explain what AI is (a system that can learn and make decisions based on data), how it works (using algorithms and machine learning), and some examples of how it is used in various industries.
- **Discuss the implications:** Once you have established a basic understanding of AI, discuss the impact of its use. This could include the potential benefits (such as increased efficiency and productivity) and potential risks (such as job displacement and ethical concerns).
- **Consider theological and ethical implications:** Church leaders may be particularly interested in AI's theological and ethical implications. Discuss how AI relates to biblical concepts such as human dignity, justice, and compassion, and consider how its use could promote or challenge these values.
- **Highlight relevant use cases:** Find examples of how AI is used in other areas relevant to the church context. For example, AI-powered chatbots can be used for pastoral care, while AI-powered analytics can help churches understand attendance and giving patterns.
- **Encourage dialogue and reflection:** Finally, encourage church leaders to engage in conversation and reflection on the ethical implications of AI and to consider how its use aligns with the values and mission of their church community.

By approaching the topic of AI in a way that is accessible, relevant, and grounded in the values and concerns of church leaders, we can help foster a deeper understanding of the potential benefits and risks of this emerging technology.

6. What are some ways I can use AI in my Church?
Here are a few examples:

Chatbots for Pastoral Care

- Chatbots are AI-powered tools that simulate human conversation and provide primary pastoral care. They can respond to prayer requests, answer questions about faith, and provide spiritual guidance. This can be especially beneficial for individuals who may not have direct access to a pastor or clergy member.

App Recommendations:

- **ChatGPT**: An AI chatbot developed by OpenAI that can understand natural language and respond to questions and comments.
- **Microsoft Bot Framework**: A comprehensive offering that you can use to build and deploy high-quality bots for your users to enjoy wherever they are talking.
- **Dialogflow**: A Google-owned developer of human-computer interaction technologies based on natural language conversations.
- **IBM Watson Assistant**: An AI assistant that learns more with less data and can be deployed on any cloud or on-premises environment.

Automated Translations

- AI-powered translation tools can help bridge language barriers in religious spaces. They can translate sermons or religious texts into different languages, making them accessible to more people.

App Recommendations:

- **Wordly**: Provides live translation into audio and captions, making church services more inclusive.
- **Google Translate**: A free service that instantly translates words, phrases, and web pages between English and over 100 other languages.
- **Microsoft Translator**: A cloud-based automatic translation service used to build applications, websites, and tools requiring multi-language support.
- **spf.io**: An AI-powered translation tool designed to make events accessible in many languages.

Smart Classrooms

- AI-powered tools can enhance religious education in classrooms. They can answer students' questions during class, provide personalized assignment feedback, and create a more engaging learning environment.

App Recommendations:

- **Kahoot:** We create, share, and play learning games or trivia quizzes in minutes.
- **Quizlet:** A mobile and web-based study application that allows students to study information via learning tools and games.
- **Edmodo:** A tool that helps connect all learners with the people and resources needed to reach their full potential.
- **Google Classroom:** A free web service developed by Google for schools that aims to simplify creating, distributing, and grading assignments.

Predictive Analytics for Church Growth

- AI-powered analytics tools can analyze data on attendance, giving, and other metrics to predict patterns of growth and decline in a church community. This can help church leaders make more informed decisions about resource allocation and future planning.

App Recommendations:

- **Gloo:** Provides churches with AI-powered tools to analyze data and improve communication channels to connect with members.
- **Church Metrics:** A free tool for tracking church data to provide insightful, actionable information
- **Breeze:** An easy-to-use church management software for small and mid-sized churches
- **Faithlife Equip:** An integrated ministry platform that combines multiple tools to help streamline church operations

Customized Worship Experiences

- AI-powered music and lighting systems can create customized worship experiences. They can adjust the tempo and style of music based on the congregation's preferences and create different moods and atmospheres during worship services.

App Recommendations:

- **Ableton Live:** A digital audio workstation for macOS and Windows that is designed for live performances as well as for composing, recording, arranging, mixing, and mastering.
- **ProPresenter:** A cross-platform presentation software for live events that allows you to create high-quality video outputs
- **EasyWorship:** A powerful yet straightforward worship presentation software that helps you create even the most complex presentations in minutes.

- **Chroma-Q**: A range of premium performance solutions for designers, including LED fixtures, moving lights, and lighting control software

7. How do we maintain a solid Christian love ethic amid AI?

Keeping a Christian Love ethic with Artificial Intelligence (AI) requires us to consider how our use of AI aligns with the values of love, compassion, and justice at the heart of Christian ethics. Here are a few fundamental principles to keep in mind:

- Human dignity: As Christians, we believe that all human beings are created in the image of God and have inherent dignity and worth. When developing and using AI, we should ensure that it respects and upholds this dignity rather than treating people as data points or objects to be analyzed.
- Justice: The biblical concept of justice emphasizes fairness, equality, and the protection of vulnerable populations. We should use AI to promote these values rather than perpetuate or exacerbate existing inequalities or biases.
- Accountability: As creators and users of AI, we are responsible for ensuring that it is being used ethically and for the benefit of all. This requires transparency, accountability, and ongoing evaluation of the ethical implications of our use of AI.
- Compassion: As Christians, we are called to love our neighbors as ourselves and to show compassion to those who are suffering. When developing and using AI, we should consider how it can promote human flourishing and alleviate suffering.
- Humility: Finally, we should approach the development and use of AI with humility, recognizing that our knowledge and understanding are limited and that we cannot fully anticipate all of the ethical implications of our use of AI. This requires ongoing dialogue, reflection, and a willingness to listen to diverse perspectives and feedback.
-

By keeping these principles in mind, we can use AI in ways consistent with a Christian Love ethic, promoting the flourishing of all people and creation.

13. FUTURE CHURCH TRENDS

The Sons of Issachar saw the "Signs of the Times." (1 Chron 12:32)

Ezekiel looked for those who would, 'Stand in the gap.' (Ezekiel 22:30)

Jesus said we would do 'Greater works" (John 14:12)

Welcome to the end! (Cue Boyz 2 Men) I wanted to end this book by projecting trends for the next 5-10 years. Yes, some of these are rooted in my thoughts. Some are cited based on our buying trends as leaders. They may not all come true, but most will. I'm excited about the future of the church. Ready? Here is the future! Join me in having a little fun.

1 - Women in Leadership - By 2030, nearly 60% of the world's wealth will be owned by women…and that is a low projection. Women must be in leadership positions. If you want to see your church expand, start positioning people in leadership based on merit not sexual organs. I guarantee you will see the entire dynamic of your church change with women making decisions. The future is female.

2 - **Black and **other races** churches will grow. Multi-Racial churches driven by white preachers will not - Too often,** "multi-cultural" churches are black/brown people assimilating to white churches and white culture. i.e. CCM/White hymnity. To a point where, as one colleague said, "members of my church as me to sing CCM believing the spirit moves more in white music than our own. When it is because CCM represents privilege, authority, and power." Over the next few years, we will see black and brown people leave white preacher-led churches for black/brown-led churches. The false sense of "unity" and "anti-racism" without an effective reading of scripture has exposed communities and cultures that want Colorful bodies for promotion, not engagement. For black churches, we must be open to new people attending, asking questions, and being "restored" after attending a church we, as leaders, disagreed with them attending.

3 - Increase in conversions
While we are not seeing droves of people come to altars and out the back door, we are witnessing a depth and care for scripture that has never been seen before. Churches will expand at Christ's pace, not our marketing.

4 - Giving will be down 20-30%
Many churches have already expressed feeling this with multiple pastors and

leaders I know either being fired or having their salaries cut without reprieve. With the loss of jobs, minimum wage increase with hour decrease, and cost of living, charitable giving is often the first to go out of the window.

5 - Pastors Leaving churches altogether.

Time with their children, spouse, and community without board intervention or hope of being paid the following week has led to a mass exodus of great leaders from good/great churches. This is a scary trend. We are losing phenomenal leadership from the Christian community not because of moral failure but because of survival.

6 - Fewer people going into ministry long term

This is a more extended range projection. The pulpit prepares you for politics. Fewer people will jump into the weight of ministry because of financial instability and theological normativity. We will see fewer people in ministry staying for 20-30 year pastorates and see 5-10 year pastorates as stepping into an area/profession more intentional to their skillset.

7 - Digital ministry is another "church."

There will be a group of people who will never return to church in person. Period. We must enrich and stabilize online ministry. They are namely, adding an entire online worship experience and staffing to make it excellent. Using an iPhone with house audio is no longer sufficient. Begin to consider your online live stream as another church with another pastor and another facility. 89% of churches currently offer in-person and online services, and 81% plan to continue doing so. This indicates that the hybrid church model, which blends in-person and online engagement, is here to stay.[23]

---

[23] Pushpay. (2023, December 27). The defining church tech trend of 2023 will be refinement. Pushpay. https://pushpay.com/blog/the-defining-church-tech-trend-of-2023-will-be-refinement/

8-VR/AR/AI web

Virtual reality (VR), Augmented Reality (AR), and Artificial Intelligence (AI) are all infused in how we shop, live, watch television, and experience the internet. As the church leans into the future, relevancy will be assimilated into these already established areas. Consider this, if Porn can have virtual reality experiences, if Pokemon and NBC can enhance experiences at home with AR, and; if websites and social media control our news through artificial intelligence, it is imperative that the church as a whole understands and makes use of what is becoming "normal." Churches have begun experimenting with AR and 3-D worship experiences. The culture of "risk-taking' must be a cultural value, not a COVID-19 throwaway. AI ran websites are not a "thought". They are a reality. Either get hit by it or lead through it.

To that end, here are some follow-ups to tech

- **Virtual Reality (VR) Services**: As pastors, we will need to create a fully online Virtual Reality Campus. The future is immersive.
- **Augmented Reality (AR) Bible Studies**: AR can bring Bible stories to life, making them more engaging and interactive. I.e. Pokemon.
- **Robotics in Church Operations**: Robots can assist with various church operations, from maintenance and cleaning to assistance during services, with a decrease in giving, an uptick in sustainability through a one-time purchase against a salary.

9 - Boomers and Millennials will drive churches

Millennials and Boomers are the largest generations. Boomers are getting closer to retirement, meaning their availability will increase. Millennials are proceeding to earn some of those empty seats at work. That means Millennial making potential will increase, and volunteering will decrease along with Boomer giving not increasing but volunteering will. It is imperative that cross-generational ministry and collaboration with correct, consistent language happens. The dynamics of our churches are about to shift drastically. Casting out one generation will destroy our churches. Not to mention—Generation Z and Generation Alpha will run our Teen, tech, and Young Adult Ministries with two years of no cultural engagement and church being an "option" to click on.

What about Gen-X? We forgot about them like we forgot about Dre.

10 - Need for spaces to teach secular theories with scripture (sexuality/CRT, etc)

Theologically engaging secular thinking is essential. Contextualizing scripture is important. Both must happen in churches. We need it to win leaders and thinkers. A complete picture of Jesus means having difficult conversations about how we have shown and will show Jesus.

So what?

If these are trends, what can we do? Here are four suggestions:

1 - Look for Giving from Community Businesses

Local community organizations and businesses have charitable and social innovation grants and monies available. Take a look at your budget, talk to the members in your church who can write grants and have great relationships, and take advantage of that situation. You will be surprised how much money is out there. Ask.

2- Be mindful of what you ingest

When we consider the increase of Prosperity preachers in the 80s, and 90's, it spilled over into many of our churches because of a lack of access to commentaries, seminaries, etc. Money speaks. The churches with the best cameras and most members are driving the theology of our people. It is so easy to succumb to what is popular. There will be an increase in popular preachers and an increase in heresy. Be mindful of your time in prayer and preparation to not fall into the trap of popularizing the gospel. Lift Jesus, and He will draw.

3 – Diversify your Skillset for Co-vocational and bi-vocational ministry

Pastors and Staff will need secular work to offset the lack of giving. This is also a challenge to seminaries and divinity schools to encourage students to have multiple layers of education, whether that is law, social work, or business. This trend is scary as churches will expect pastors to give full-time work to churches paying part-time.

4 - Collaborative ministry without Denominational guidelines

If this era has taught us anything, Denominations are more constricting than they are liberating. Denominations have been outgrown for years on Matters of race, healthcare, opening/closing, preaching, etc. Cross-denominational ministry and work are important. We are not monolithic people; we cannot make our churches monolithic.

Pandemics only accelerate life. In this case, it accelerated so many areas of the local church and revealed several of our weaknesses. By no means is the local church dead. Nor is the future going to kill it. We must seize an opportunity to be critical about ourselves, our contexts, and our motivation. Let's go!

Here are some other trends

Here are a few projections and trends that I foresee coming in 2030. Special thanks to the book *2030*.[24]

Birthplace of the next industrial revolution: sub-Saharan Africa

- The reason: 500 million acres of fertile yet undeveloped agricultural land
- The size of Mexico: 500 million acres
- Percentage of the world's wealth owned by women in 2000: 15
- Percentage of the world's wealth owned by women in 2030: 55
- If Lehman Brothers had been Lehman Sisters: global financial crisis averted.

- Worldwide, the number of people who went hungry in 2017:
- 821 million
- Worldwide, the number of people who will go hungry in 2030 200 million
- Worldwide, the number of people who were obese in 2017:
- 650 million
- Worldwide, the number of people who will be obese in 2030:
  - o billion
- Percentage of Americans projected to be obese in 2030:
- 50
- Percentage of the world's land occupied by cities in 2030: 1.1
- Percentage of the world's population living in cities in 2030: 60
- Percentage of worldwide carbon emissions produced by cities in 2030: 87

---

[24] *Source: Guillén, Mauro F. "2030: How Today's Biggest Trends Will Collide and Reshape the Future of Everything." Hardcover, August 25, 2020.*

- Percentage of world's urban population exposed to rising sea levels in 2030: 80

- The largest middle-class consumer market today: United States and Western Europe
- The largest middle-class consumer market in 2030: China
- By 2030, the number of people entering the middle class in emerging markets: 1 billion
- The number of people currently in the middle class in the United States: 223 million
- The number of people in the middle class in the United States in 2030: 209 million

For Every baby born in the US, 4.4 are being born in China, 6.5 in India, and 10.2 in Africa. Projected 450 Million babies born in Africa by 2030

Want more AI/
Follow @ThatTechPastor

the church of ai

END.

That's all! Thanks for reading. I cannot stand long drawn out conclusions because, *It's So Hard to Say Goodbye.* If you want to learn more about AI and my perspective, check out my IG @ThatTechPastor and my website www.jrlester.com where I have a masterclass on how to add AI to your church community.

May God himself, the God of peace, sanctify you through and through. May your whole spirit, soul and body be kept blameless at the coming of our Lord Jesus Christ. The one who calls you is faithful, and he will do it. (1 Thess. 5:23-24)

Go build the kingdom.

GLOSSARY OF TERMS:

Adaptation: The process by which AI-enabled robots become more responsive to changing conditions and user preferences, typically involving the ability to sense, analyze, and respond appropriately to environmental stimuli.

AI (Artificial Intelligence): The simulation of human intelligence processes by computer systems, particularly the ability to learn from data, reason, understand natural language, and perceive its environment.

AI Policy: A set of guidelines, principles, and frameworks established by an organization to govern the development, deployment, and use of artificial intelligence systems in a responsible, ethical, and compliant manner.

Algorithm: A formula or set of formal rules, logical operations, instructions for getting a result from input elements. In AI, the algorithm tells the machine how to go about finding answers to a question or solutions to a problem.

Analytical Intelligence: The ability to process information for problem-solving and learning from it. This intelligence involves taking in and sorting information, logical reasoning, and mathematical processing.

Artificial Intelligence (AI): Refers to the simulation of human intelligence processes by machines, especially computer systems. AI encompasses tasks such as learning, reasoning, problem-solving, perception, and language understanding.

Automation: The use of technology to perform tasks or processes with minimal human intervention, often involving the application of AI and robotics to streamline operations and increase efficiency.

Autonomous: Autonomy is the ability to act independently of an external ruling authority. In AI, a machine or a vehicle is referred to as autonomous if it does not require input from a human operator to function properly.

Big Data: Large amounts of structured and unstructured data that are too complex to be handled by standard data processing software. Big data can help companies optimize their processes, determine trends, and address customers in a targeted fashion.

Chatbots: Computer programs designed to simulate conversation with human users, typically used in customer service, information delivery, and interactive experiences.

Classification: A specific algorithm technique that allows machines to assign categories to data points. An example of a classification task is for a credit card company to decide, based on information about an applicant's income, age, employment, and debt repaying history, if the applicant has good, bad, or mixed credit.

Clustering: A specific algorithm technique that allows machines to group similar data into larger data categories. An example of a clustering task is to group words that frequently occur together in the context of presidential speeches.

Competence: The skills, knowledge, abilities, and attributes required to perform tasks, duties, and responsibilities effectively within a particular domain or context, including proficiency in traditional practices and adaptability to emerging technologies.

Continuous Learning: Ongoing process of acquiring, updating, and expanding knowledge, skills, and capabilities over time. Continuous learning emphasizes the importance of lifelong education, professional development, and adaptation to changing environments to stay relevant and effective.

Convolutional Neural Networks (CNN): A type of artificial neural network, commonly used in image recognition and processing, that applies convolutional filters to input data to extract features.

Creative Accumulation: A strategy for dealing with competence disruption that involves preserving old knowledge while adding new knowledge in a creative and innovative manner to adapt to changing circumstances and technologies.

Customer Experience: The overall experience a customer has with a product, service, or brand throughout the entire customer journey, including interactions before, during, and after the purchase.

Customer Strategy: The plan and approach a company adopts to attract, retain, and satisfy customers, typically involving marketing, sales, and customer service initiatives.

Data Collection and Analysis: The process of gathering and examining data to uncover insights, trends, and patterns that can inform decision-making and drive business strategies, often facilitated by AI technologies.

Data Mining: The process of sorting through large sets of data to identify recurring patterns through classification, clustering, among other algorithms, with the goal of extracting useful information to solve a given problem.

Datafication: The process of transforming everyday activities and processes into data by monitoring and tracking them, thus quantifying, visualizing, analyzing, and even predicting previously unconscious or unseen aspects of life. An example is counting the number of steps taken in a day.

Deep Learning: A subset of machine learning where artificial neural networks, inspired by the structure and function of the human brain, learn from large amounts of data.

Diffusion Models: Models used in generative AI for image generation, which add random noise to images and then remove the noise to generate new outputs.

Digitalization: Refers to using digital technologies and tools to optimize internal processes, expanding or reinventing business models based on technological innovations, and incorporating changes in society and different sectors. Digitalization also means digital transformation, a process that takes a holistic perspective.

Digitization: Refers generally to a purely technical process of transferring information from analog to digital form. For example, digitizing old paper photographs by scanning them.

Disruption: The process by which established industries, practices, or technologies are fundamentally altered or replaced by innovative new approaches, often driven by advancements in AI, robotics, or other emerging technologies.

Disruptive Innovation: Process or phenomenon through which new products, services, or technologies disrupt existing markets, business models, or value networks by offering superior benefits, addressing unmet needs, or creating new value propositions.

Electricity Grid: A network of transmission lines, substations, and transformers used to deliver electricity from power plants to consumers, allowing for the distribution and supply of electrical energy across regions or countries.

Emerging Technology: Novel innovations or advancements that are new or relatively new and have the potential to significantly impact or change various aspects of society, industry, or daily life. Emerging technologies can include products, services, processes, or concepts that offer new benefits or capabilities.

Empathetic Intelligence: The ability to recognize, understand, and respond to the emotions of oneself and others, involving skills such as empathy, compassion, active listening, and emotional regulation.

Environment, Social, and Governance (ESG): Framework used to evaluate and measure the sustainability and societal impact of businesses, investments, or operations based on environmental, social, and governance criteria. ESG considerations address factors such as environmental conservation, social responsibility, human rights, diversity, ethics, and corporate governance practices.

Ethical Considerations: The evaluation and integration of moral principles, values, and ethical standards into the development, deployment, and use of AI systems to ensure fairness, transparency, accountability, and respect for human dignity.

Ethics: The branch of philosophy concerned with moral principles, values, and standards of conduct that guide individuals' behaviors and interactions, as well as the evaluation of what is right or wrong, good or bad, in various situations.

Generative AI: A type of artificial intelligence focused on creating new content, such as text, images, or even code, based on patterns and data it has been trained on.

GPT-4: A deep learning system that can generate natural language texts on almost any topic given some input or prompt. GPT-4 can write stories, essays, code lyrics, tweets, and more.

Human-Centric View of AI: A perspective that emphasizes human control and oversight over the development, deployment, and use of artificial intelligence systems, ensuring alignment with ethical principles, values, and societal norms.

Implementation: The process of putting a plan or system into effect, including the execution of strategies, methods, or technologies to achieve desired outcomes.

Industrial Revolution: A period of significant technological, economic, and social transformation characterized by the widespread adoption of mechanized manufacturing processes, steam power, and the development of new industries, which began in the late 18th century and continued into the early 19th century.

Innovation: The process of introducing new ideas, methods, products, or services that create value, address unmet needs, solve problems, or improve existing processes, practices, or technologies.

Innovative Approaches: Novel methods, strategies, or techniques that challenge conventional thinking or practices and lead to the development of new solutions, products, or services to address emerging challenges or opportunities.

Internet of Things (IoT): A network of interconnected devices, sensors, and objects embedded with technology that enables them to collect, exchange, and analyze data, as well as communicate and interact with each other and with other systems or users over the internet.

Interpretability: The degree to which the decisions or outputs of AI systems can be understood, explained, or interpreted by humans, including the transparency, comprehensibility, and trustworthiness of the underlying algorithms and processes.

Knowledge Graphs: Graph-based knowledge representation structures that organize and interconnect information in a semantic network, enabling machines to understand, reason about, and retrieve knowledge in a more human-like manner.

Machine Learning: A subset of artificial intelligence that focuses on the development of algorithms and statistical models that enable computers to learn and improve their performance on a specific task or domain through experience, data analysis, and iterative optimization processes.

Natural Language Processing (NLP): A branch of artificial intelligence that deals with the interaction between computers and humans using natural language, enabling machines to understand, interpret, and generate human language.

Neural Networks: A set of algorithms, modeled loosely after the human brain, that are designed to recognize patterns. They interpret sensory data through a kind of machine perception, labeling, or clustering raw input.

Personalization: The process of tailoring products, services, experiences, or communications to individual preferences, interests, behaviors, or characteristics, often facilitated by data analytics, machine learning, and customer insights.

Predictive Analytics: The use of data, statistical algorithms, and machine learning techniques to identify patterns and predict future outcomes or behaviors, enabling organizations to anticipate trends, make informed decisions, and optimize strategies.

Privacy Concerns: The ethical and legal considerations related to the collection, storage, use, and sharing of personal data, including issues of consent, transparency, data protection, and individual rights to privacy and data security.

Quantum Computing: A type of computing that takes advantage of the quantum state of subatomic particles to perform operations on data, potentially offering exponentially faster processing speeds and greater computational power than classical computing systems.

Reinforcement Learning: A type of machine learning where an agent learns to make decisions by taking actions in an environment to maximize cumulative rewards or minimize negative consequences, guided by feedback or reinforcement signals.

Responsible AI: The practice of developing, deploying, and using artificial intelligence systems in a manner that is ethical, transparent, fair, inclusive, and respectful of human rights and values, with a focus on minimizing potential harms and maximizing societal benefits.

Robotics: The interdisciplinary field of engineering and science that involves the design, construction, operation, and use of robots, as well as the study of their sensory feedback, environmental interactions, and autonomous or semi-autonomous behaviors.

Self-Driving Cars: Autonomous vehicles equipped with sensors, cameras, and artificial intelligence systems that enable them to navigate and operate safely on roads without human intervention, potentially revolutionizing transportation and mobility.

Sustainability: The ability to meet the needs of the present without compromising the ability of future generations to meet their own needs, encompassing economic, environmental, and social dimensions of development and resource management.

System Optimization: The process of improving the performance, efficiency, reliability, scalability, or cost-effectiveness of a system, process, or operation through analysis, modeling, experimentation, and iterative refinement.

Technology Adoption: The process by which individuals, organizations, or societies accept and integrate new technologies into their daily lives, workflows, or practices, typically influenced by factors such as perceived usefulness, ease of use, compatibility, and perceived risks or benefits.

Transparency: The principle of openness, visibility, and accountability in decision-making processes, operations, and communications, including the disclosure of information, intentions, motives, and outcomes to relevant stakeholders.

Unsupervised Learning: A type of machine learning where the algorithm learns patterns from input data without labeled responses, allowing it to explore and discover hidden structures or relationships in the data.

User Experience (UX): The overall experience of a person using a product, system, or service, encompassing aspects such as usability, accessibility, ease of use, satisfaction, and emotional engagement, as well as the user's perceptions, behaviors, and interactions throughout the interaction lifecycle.

User Interface (UI): The visual, interactive, and functional elements of a digital product, system, or interface that enable users to interact with and control it, including menus, buttons, forms, navigation controls, and other graphical elements.

Virtual Reality (VR): A computer-generated simulation or immersive environment that allows users to interact with and experience artificial three-dimensional worlds or environments as if they were physically present, typically using head-mounted displays and motion-tracking technology.

Visualization: The graphical representation of data, information, or concepts to facilitate understanding, analysis, exploration, communication, or decision-making, typically involving charts, graphs, diagrams, maps, or interactive visual interfaces.

WORK'S CITED

(in order of appearance)

Edinburgh Futures Institute. (n.d.). Understanding AI from a Theological Perspective. Retrieved from https://efi.ed.ac.uk/understanding-ai-from-a-theological-perspective/

Webb, A. (2019). The Big Nine: How the Tech Titans and Their Thinking Machines Could Warp Humanity (p. 50). New York: Public Affairs.

Harari, Y. N. (2017). Homo Deus: A Brief History of Tomorrow (pp. 386-387). New York: HarperCollins.

Levy, S. (2017, October 17). God Is a Bot, and Anthony Levandowski Is His Messenger. Wired. Retrieved from https://www.wired.com/story/god-is-a-bot-and-anthony-levandowski-is-his-messenger/

Barna Group. (2016, May 1.). Churchless Cities: Where Does Your City Rank? Retrieved from https://www.barna.com/research/churchless-cities-where-does-your-city-rank/

Alamy. (n.d.). C. H. Spurgeon. Retrieved from https://www.alamy.com/stock-photo/c-h-spurgeon.html?sortBy=relevant

Deezer. (n.d.). [Artist Name]. Retrieved from https://www.deezer.com/us/artist/195755

Joshua Project. (n.d.). People Groups Statistics. Retrieved from https://joshuaproject.net/people_groups/statistics

Enablers of Change. (n.d.). What Are the Factors That Affect Adoption? Retrieved from https://www.enablersofchange.com.au/what-are-the-factors-that-affect-adoption/

The Bold Business Expert. (2020, November 2). Diffusion of Innovation: Getting Past the First Wave of Innovators and Early Adopters to Reach the Tipping Point. Retrieved from https://theboldbusinessexpert.com/2020/11/02/diffusion-of-innovation-getting-past-the-first-wave-of-innovators-and-early-adopters-to-reach-the-tipping-point/

Rogers, E. M. (n.d.). Detailed review of Rogers' diffusion of innovations theory and educational technology-related studies based on Rogers' theory. Retrieved from https://www.researchgate.net/publication/284675572_Detailed_review_of_Rogers'_diffusion_of_innovations_theory_and_educational_technology-related_studies_based_on_Rogers'_theory

IEEE Spectrum. (n.d.). Dartmouth AI Workshop. Retrieved from https://spectrum.ieee.org/dartmouth-ai-workshop

Rich, E., & Knight, K. (1991). Artificial Intelligence. New Delhi: McGraw-Hill.

The Guardian. (2023, February 2). ChatGPT surpasses 100 million users as OpenAI's fastest-growing app. Retrieved from https://www.theguardian.com/technology/2023/feb/02/chatgpt-100-million-users-open-ai-fastest-growing-app

Economy App. (2024, February 19). ChatGPT reached 100M users in 2 months...

Retrieved from
https://twitter.com/EconomyApp/status/1622029832099082241?ref=as
semblyai.com

Kyle, P. (2021, September 19). New technology is always scary. Medium. Retrieved from https://medium.com/pronouncedkyle/new-technology-is-always-scary-8bf977a13773

Goodwin Law. (2023, April 12). US Artificial Intelligence Regulations: Watch List for 2023. Retrieved from https://www.goodwinlaw.com/en/insights/publications/2023/04/04_12-us-artificial-intelligence-regulations

International Association of Privacy Professionals (IAPP). (2023, November). US federal AI governance: Laws, policies and strategies. Retrieved from https://iapp.org/resources/article/us-federal-ai-governance/

Thomson Reuters. (2024, February 11). Legalweek 2024: Current US AI regulation means adopting a strategic — and communicative — approach. Retrieved from https://www.thomsonreuters.com/en-us/posts/legal/legalweek-2024-ai-regulation/

Huang, M. H., & Rust, R. T. (2018). A theory of job transformation. Artificial Intelligence in Service. Journal of Service Research, 21(2), 155-172.

Pushpay. (2023, December 27). The defining church tech trend of 2023 will be refinement. Retrieved from https://pushpay.com/blog/the-defining-church-tech-trend-of-2023-will-be-refinement/

Guillén, M. F. (2020). 2030: How Today's Biggest Trends Will Collide and Reshape the Future of Everything. Hardcover.

ABOUT THE AUTHOR

Dr. Justin R. Lester is a man of many talents. He is an author, speaker, and pastor at Friendship Baptist Church in Vallejo, California. He earned his Bachelor's degree from Marquette University, his Master's degree from Vanderbilt University, and his Doctorate in Ministry from Boston University.

In addition to his pastoral duties, Dr. Lester is a decisive non-profit leader with a proven history of improving operations and boosting financial health and company sustainability through adaptive leadership. He is also a higher education professional with a focus on Black Religious Leadership, Practical Theology, and Communication Strategy.

Dr. Lester is passionate about living a full life, and he loves his son, wife, and coffee. He has written several books, including *Let's Play Church,* which examines the role of the church in modern society, and *Necessary Endings,* which explores the importance of letting go of things that are holding us back.

Dr. Lester is a sought-after speaker and has appeared on numerous podcasts and in the news media. He is available to participate in your story, whether that means talking, preaching, or simply enjoying a cup of coffee together.

Web: www.jrlester.com
Social: @ThatTechPastor

Made in the USA
Las Vegas, NV
30 March 2024

88043506R00085